THE

JOURNEY

By Marian Brogen

Copyright © 2022 by Marian Brogen. All rights reserved. No part of this publication may be reproduced, stored in a retrieval system, or transmitted in any way by any means, electronic, mechanical, photocopy, recording, or otherwise without the prior permission of the author except as provided by USA copyright law.

Scripture quotations marked "NIV" are taken from the Holy Bible, New International Version ®, Copyright © 1973, 1978, 1984 by International Bible Society. Used by permission of Zondervan Publishing House. All rights reserved.

Scripture quotations marked "NKJV" are taken from *The New King James Version* / Thomas Nelson Publishers, Nashville: Thomas Nelson Publishers. Copyright © 1982. Used by permission. All rights reserved.

This narrative is a work of non-fiction. However, names, descriptions, entities, and incidents included herein are based on actual events, locations, and the lives of real people. In the interest of security and privacy, some names and descriptors may have been changed. Any resemblance to actual persons, places, incidents, or entities is purely coincidental.

This book is designed to provide accurate and authoritative information about the subject matter covered. This information is given with the understanding that the author is NOT engaged in rendering legal, professional, or personal advice. Should you find that your situation(s) may be similar to those described in this work, the details of your situation remain fact dependent upon your specific circumstances. For accurate and relevant counsel, please seek the services of a competent professional.

Table of Contents

HAPPINESS	1
The Love Of God	5
Salvation Questions	13
Water Baptism	19
Water Baptism Questions	23
Prayer	29
Prayer Questions	35
Study The Bible	39
Study Questions	43
The Armor of God	47
Armour of God Questions	57
Baptism in the Holy Spirit	63
Holy Spirit Questions	67
Beauty Of A Woman	71
Beauty Review	79
The Christian Marriage	83
The Opposite Of The Proverbs 31 Woman	89
Ten Commandments For Those Who Have Been Previously Married	99
The Christian Marriage Review	101
Healing	111
Trust:	119
The Words We Speak	123
THE JOURNEY	135

HAPPINESS

*From the beginning of our lives, we are in search of happiness.
Our nature yearns for it. As young children, our parents did all they could to make us happy, sometimes unwisely.
We learned how to manipulate our parents into giving us the things we wanted whether it was good for us or not.
Then when we obtained those things, after a short time we lost interest in them and began to look for something new.*

*This sets a pattern for our lives. As we mature into adulthood we find ourselves again looking at life in the same way.
We have the misconception that a good job, money, and status will bring us happiness but that is the furthest from the truth.
You may think you have found that special someone, live in the fanciest house, drive the sportiest car, and have all the money you will ever need at your disposal, and still feel a void in your life.*

What if all these things were gone tomorrow, how would you feel?

We can look to man, to money, and things as our source of happiness but only when you find the Lord and walk daily with Him will you feel the peace and joy, and happiness that our nature craves.

*Always remember that God is our source for **all** things.
So stop looking at man for your happiness.
We need only to look inward and upward to find the happiness we so desire.*

It was a Tuesday evening in 1998 when I first met Eva Thomas when she came to a women's prayer meeting at my church. She came in after the session started and sat in the back row. It wasn't until she came forward for prayer that I noticed her. We all gathered around her and prayed with her not knowing the trauma she had experienced in her life. The Lord laid on my heart that I needed to help her. I invited her and she came to my Sunday School class the next Sunday. This was the beginning of a wonderful friendship.

As we began to get to know each other I was amazed at how terrible her life had become, and the things she had to endure at the hands of others. It wasn't until she surrendered her life to the Lord that her healing begin. She had been living in a very dark place but when she allowed Jesus to help her, things began to change. It was a slow process but one by one she faced her fears. Over the years she had written journals as a way of expressing her pain. We took those journals and wrote the book called Woman of Victory. She started a ministry under that name which is centered around single mothers. She's an amazing woman whom God has used multiple times to help others.

This workbook, THE JOURNEY, is based on some of the teachings I shared with Eva.

In her book, Eva shares the journey she has taken to be free from the pain and hurt from her past. I pray it will help you to grow closer to the Lord and help you to overcome the battles you are facing in your life.

My Journal

The Love Of God

What is love? That's a hard question to answer.

As children, we love our parents, and we believe they love us. As a sister, we love our siblings, but they can be annoying. As we get older we begin to fall in love with people we hope will love us back and eventually marry. As we become mothers that love is very strong towards our children, but it's not easy to put into words what these kinds of love mean to us.

As children we look to our parents for guidance, we want them to be proud of our accomplishments, etc. We find a way to wrap them around our fingers so we can get what we want from them whether it's good for us or not. And if we don't get our way we throw tantrums and do whatever we can so we can get what we want.
If we have brothers and sisters we can become very selfish with our toys etc. and blame them for anything that goes wrong.
As adults, we yearn to fall in love hoping it becomes a love that will last for all time. And as we have children, that love we feel can overwhelm us.
Throughout our lives, we learn how to manipulate those around us. I'm not proud of the fact that I've done these things. I think most of us have at some time in our lives.
But there is a love that is greater than anything we can ever imagine, and that's God's love, the love that He has for us. It's all-encompassing love. Something that is hard to understand. We are not perfect people, we mess up every day. We think things we shouldn't think, we speak words we shouldn't say, and we do things we shouldn't do. Many times we think only of ourselves and not what we are doing to others. But through all this, we can be assured that God loves us. He doesn't always like what we do or why we do the things we do but He loves us anyway. He shed His blood and died for us so we would have the opportunity to ask for forgiveness and to spend the rest of our days with Him. We cannot fathom this kind of love because we are not able to love that way.

Psalms 100:5 NIV
'For the Lord is good and His love endures forever, His faithfulness continues through all generations.'

Psalms 103:11 NIV
'For as high as the heavens are above the earth, so great is His love for those who fear Him'

Can you imagine loving someone like that?? We get so wrapped up in people's lives that the only things we see are their faults.

We don't deserve the kind of love that God has for us but I'm so grateful that He can look past our faults and love us anyway.

Loving someone opens the door for hurt and disappointment to come into our lives. It doesn't always happen but many times it's in the back of our minds. We're always waiting for something bad to happen.

Now put yourself in God's place. He created us and we are made in His image. He wants the very best for us, but we are so ungrateful and couldn't care less what we think of Him. We use His name in such a way that we start cursing others, it's just another name, no big deal. From the beginning of time, people have been disobedient and had to suffer the consequences of His anger. Yes, God gets angry. He sent His Son Jesus to this earth to pay the penalty for our disobedience. Jesus suffered terribly. He was beaten, spit upon, and had a crown of thorns pushed into his skull. His hands and feet were nailed to the cross and hung there while people cursed Him. And He experienced all this so that we would have the opportunity of forgiveness. It's sad to say but every day He suffers when He sees His children live ungodly lives. Every time we cause grief to others or even to ourselves it's like slapping Him in the face. We spend so much time living like the world lives that there is very little to separate us.
Are you loving God? Have you asked Him to forgive all the wrong you have done? Are you ready to set aside the old you and put on the new you? When we ask God to forgive our sins He washes all our past hurts and disappointments away. He washes all of our sins away then He remembers them no more.

Hebrew 8:12 NIV
'For I will forgive their wickedness and will remember their sins no more'

Now you know that God loves you unconditionally are you ready to take that next step?

Salvation.

Luke 19:1-10 *tells the story of Zacchaeus, a wealthy tax collector who wanted to see Jesus. Because of the crowd and being small in stature, he decided to climb a sycamore tree to see Him. When Jesus reached the tree He called Zacchaeus by name and said He wanted to stay at his house. (Jesus knows us by name, and He knows where we are and what's going on in our lives).*

Because of his dishonesty in collecting taxes, Zacchaeus realized he needed to change his ways and right there he repented of his sins.

*Millions of people throughout the ages have heard the **Salvation** message but only the ones who respond; who repent and believe, will be the ones to inherit the Kingdom of God.*

John 3:3
'Jesus replied, "Very truly I tell you, no one can see the kingdom of God unless they are born again.' NIV

God has chosen YOU to save.

Matthew 22:14 NIV
'For many are invited but few are chosen'

Everything in life hinges around the question 'Who is Jesus to you?' He must be your Savior and your God. The battle between God and Satan isn't just about good v. evil. But about who we choose to belong to, either God or Satan. We choose where we will spend eternity, either in Heaven or Hell. It's our choice. We choose every day which master we will serve. Your decision will affect the rest of your life.

If you have never repented of your sins now would be the time to do so.

There are just 3 things you must do to be saved:

Believe – Repent – Confess

1. Believe -
   John 3:36 NKJV
   'He who believes in the Son has everlasting life; and he who does not believe the Son shall not see life, but the wrath of God abides on him.'

   We must believe that Jesus is who God says He is:

   a) Born of a virgin.
   b) Died for our sins.
   c) Rose again from the dead.
   d) Sits at the right hand of the Father.
   e) Intercedes for us.
   f) Is coming back soon to get us.

Do you believe these statements? To believe this demands FAITH. This faith means having confidence in and believing in God. Your faith in Jesus Christ is the first step to salvation.

2. Repent -
   Mark 1:15 NIV
   'The time has come' Jesus says, 'the Kingdom of God has come near. Repent and believe the good news.'

The basic meaning of repentance is 'to turn around.' It is a turning away from evil ways and a turning to Christ and through Him to God.

People may say, 'I'm a good person, why must I be saved?' the bible tells us in

Romans 3:23 NIV
'For all have sinned and fall short of the glory of God.'
We are all sinners in need of forgiveness

Romans 6:23 NIV
'For the wages of sin is death but the gift of God is eternal life in Christ Jesus Our Lord.'

John 3:16 - 17 NIV
'For God so loved the world that He gave His one and only Son that whoever believes in Him shall not perish but have eternal life.
For God did not send His Son into the world to condemn the world but to save the world through Him.'

God came to save us not to condemn us.

3. Confess -
  1 John 1:9 NIV
  'If we confess our sins, He is faithful and just and will forgive us our sins and purify us from all unrighteousness'

Confess and He will forgive

Romans 10:10 NIV
'For it is with your heart that you believe and are justified, and it is with your mouth that you profess your faith and are saved.'

God is waiting for you to make that decision.

Pray this prayer and truly believe it in your heart :

Father, I come to You just as I am. I confess that I am a sinner needing forgiveness. I believe that Jesus is the Son of God, that He took my sin upon Himself and died on the cross for me. And I believe that He was raised from the dead and has given me power over the enemy. I ask you now to forgive me of my sins and cleanse me with your shed blood. I invite you to come and live in my heart and be the Lord of my life.

Thank you, Lord, for your love and your mercy.

In Jesus' name, Amen.

You have just made the most important decision of your life and the Bible tells us in

2 Cor 5:17 NKJV
'Therefore, if anyone is in Christ, he is a new creation, old things have passed away, behold, all things become new.'

So now we know that by accepting Christ as our Savior we are a changed person. There are probably areas in your life you will want to change. These changes will not happen overnight, it is a gradual transformation.

Matthew 18:3 NIV
'Jesus says, 'Truly I tell you, unless you change and become like little children you will never enter the Kingdom of Heaven.'

The change Jesus is talking about is being humble [not having a proud attitude], willing to be dependent on and ready to be molded by your Heavenly Father. God wants to change you, but He is only able to do so if you will allow Him to be the Lord of your life. You are starting life over

Since we know that Jesus is with us always we must remember that He knows when things go wrong in our lives. He will comfort us when we are hurting and strengthen us when Satan attacks. He will help us overcome <u>all</u> our unwanted habits. And do not forget that we have a direct line to God through prayer. He gives us wonderful peace in our hearts, and you will have the desire to share God with others.

You will have some resistance to these changes that you want to make. You once belonged to Satan but after salvation, you have become a child of God. Satan will not sit back and allow you to live your new life without some opposition. Your life circumstances will be hard at times, and for a while it may be worse than it was before you were saved. But we must not give in to the Devil.

You must stand firm in Jesus and know that He will see you through all your problems. Don't keep these problems to yourself; tell someone so they can pray with you.

It's important to surround yourself with Christian people and make Christian friends.

Now you are saved you are a witness for Christ. You will want to share Jesus with your unsaved friends, that's normal, but you cannot go back to your old ways.

Your friends need to see a change in every part of your life. How can you win them to the Lord if you continue in the same way as you did before you were saved?

You may need to be aware of the way you dress, be more modest, and not as enticing toward others. What kind of music are you listening to and what are you watching on T.V. Do they have bad language, sexual content, or violence in them? All these negative things surround us daily. We become desensitized by what we see and hear.

You may be tempted at times to fall back into your old lifestyle especially if things begin to go wrong. People may try to change your mind about God. but you must not listen to them. Keep trusting in the Lord and He will help you grow stronger every day.

Jesus is now living in you so what you see, He sees. And what you hear He hears. And where you go, He goes. As you become aware of these worldly influences it is up to you to be disciplined and walk away from the old ways.

Salvation Questions

1. Is there anyone who has not sinned? **Romans 3:10** (6th book in N.T)

----

2. Aren't good, moral people an exception? **Romans 3:23** (6Th book in N.T)

----

3. What about people who seem to do good? **Isaiah 53:6** (23rd book in O.T)

----

4. If we are all sinners; how do we know God really loves us? **Romans 5:8** (6t book in N.T)

----

5. How did God show His love for us? **John 3:16** (4th book in N.T)

----

6. What did Jesus tell Nicodemus a man had to do in order to enter Heaven? **John 3:3** (4th book in N.T)

----

7. How does one accept Jesus as his Savior? **Romans 10:9 & 10** (6th book in the N.T)

Verse 9:_____

Verse 10:_____

8. What happens when we are born again and become a Christian?
2 Corinthians 5:17 (8th book in the N.T)

_____

9. What has God promised to those who reject Him? *Romans 6:23* (6th book in N.T)

_____

10. What has He promised to those who accept Him? *Romans 6:23* (6th book in N.T)

_____

11. How can I know that I am saved? *1 John 1:9* (23rd book in N.T)

_____

12. What did we do that the sinner didn't do that makes us a Christian? *John 1:12* (4th book in N.T)

a) _____

Then what did God do for us?

b) He gave_____God

13. What is His promise to those who hear His Word and believe? *John 5:24* (4th book in N.T)

_____

14. What personal assurance does God give us so that we know we are saved? **Romans** *8:16 (6ᵗʰ book in N.T)*

Memorize: **Romans** *3:23   1 John 1:9*

My Journal

Water Baptism

I was a new Christian when I was told I needed to be baptized. I was obedient but I didn't have a clue what it was or why I needed to do it. It wasn't until a long time later did I understand what it was all about and the significance of each step a Christian must take to become stronger in the Lord. That is the reason I have a heart for the new Christians, to help them understand how to grow in their faith and develop a deeper relationship with the Lord God.

God's goal for every person is that they accept Jesus as their Savior and Lord. To repent of their sins. Jesus laid down His life so we could be saved. Salvation by itself is enough to get us into Heaven but we should not settle just for that. Jesus expects us to progress and grow beyond the initial conversion.

We should pattern our lives after Him.

Matthew 3: 15 - 16 NIV
'Jesus replied, 'Let it be so now, it is proper for us to do this to fulfill all righteousness.' Then John consented
And as soon as Jesus was baptized, He went up out of the water. At that moment Heaven was opened, and He saw the Spirit of God descending like a dove and alighting on Him.'

Water baptism is the 2nd step of your Christian life. All those who have accepted Jesus as Lord should be baptized.

Acts 22:16 NIV
'And now what are you waiting for? Get up, be baptized, and wash your sins away, calling on His name.'

Water baptism is an outward sign and testimony of our receiving Christ as Lord and Savior and of the washing away of our sins.
When undertaken with a sincere heart of faith and commitment to Jesus as Lord and Savior, is a means of receiving grace (mercy, blessings) from Christ.

Baptism can be done wherever there is enough water - a creek, swimming pool, etc. I know a pastor who was baptized in his swimming pool. You can also be baptized in a church. Jesus was baptized in the Jordan river and all scripture states He went down into the water.

Mark 1:10
'Just as Jesus was coming up out of the water, He saw heaven being torn open and the Spirit descending on Him like a dove.'

Most church baptisms are done in a baptistry where the person is immersed in water. It signifies an end to a life of sin and the beginning of a new life in Christ. That the old sinner is dead and now buried in water. Therefore, water baptism involves a commitment to a lifelong practice of turning one's back on the world and all that is evil and living a new life in the Spirit that reflects God's standards of righteousness.

You are now the property of Christ and have a share in His life, His Spirit, and His inheritance with God.

After the death and resurrection of Jesus, we find Peter (one of His disciples) preaching to the people

Acts 2:37 - 38
When the people heard this, they were cut to the heart and said to Peter and the other Apostles, 'Brothers, what shall we do?' Peter replied, 'Repent and be baptized every one of you, in the name of Jesus Christ for the forgiveness of your sins and you will receive the gift of the Holy Spirit.'

Peter had just preached his first message after being filled with the Holy Spirit. 3000 people heard Peter's message and wanted to be saved. They asked the same questions we ask today, 'What must we do to be saved?' Peter's reply is 'Repent and be baptized.'

You can be baptised anytime even immediately after salvation.

***Acts 8: 26 - 38** tells the story of Philip (who was a disciple of Jesus Christ) and a Eunuch. Philip explains the scriptures that the eunuch was* reading, the eunuch gave his heart to God and wanted to be baptized right then.

v. 38. Then both Philip and the Eunuch went down into the water and Philip baptized him.'

After Christ died and rose from the dead He gathered his disciples together and gave them this great commission.

Matthew 28:18-20 NIV
'Then Jesus came to them and said, 'All authority in heaven and on earth has been given to Me.
Therefore go and make disciples of all nations, baptizing them in the name of the Father and of the Son and of the Holy Spirit,
And teaching them to obey everything I have commanded. And surely I am with you always, to the very end of the age.'

This commission is also for us today. We should share Jesus with all our family and friends. Not all will want to hear, and it may be uncomfortable for you at times, but you are being obedient to the Lord. You may never know the impact you are making in someone's life. You are planting seeds of hopefulness, the next person who ministers to them may just water that seed and another may reap the harvest of that seed. All God wants is for us to be faithful to Him and show the love we have for others by sharing with them the Lord.

Water Baptism Questions

1. What reason for baptism did Jesus give John the Baptist? **Matthew 3:15** (1st book in N.T)

_____

2. What are we to do before being baptized? Acts (5th book in N.T)

Acts 2:38 _____

Acts 16:31 _____

3. What was the great commission Jesus gave the world before He went to Heaven? **Matthew 28: 16 - 20** (1st book in N.T)

_____

4. In the New Testament church how soon were they baptized after they became believers? (5th book in NT)

Acts 22:16_____

Acts 16:33_____

5. On the day of Pentecost what did Peter command the people to do as soon as they had repented? **Acts 2:38** (5th book in NT)

_____

6. How many were baptized on the Day Of Pentecost? **Acts 2:41** (5th book in NT)

7. Water baptism is a public act of obedience and faith. What other action does Jesus expect of those who received baptism? **Matthew 28:20** *(1ˢᵗ book in NT)*

_____

8. What are the consequences for those who do not believe in Jesus Christ? **Mark 16:16** *(2ⁿᵈ book in NT)*

_____

My Journal

Prayer

Now you have decided to follow Christ it's important to know how to communicate with Him.

The only way that any relationship can be strong is if there is clear communication between the parties. God desires to have a personal relationship with you. That's why you were created. Adam and Eve were made to worship God. He would visit them daily - what a great opportunity - hanging around with your friend God!

Prayer should be an important part of our lives. How can God meet our needs and how will we know what God's will is for our lives if we don't talk to Him? Listening to Him is just as important. So make time to do both.

James 5:16 NIV
'The prayer of a righteous person is powerful and effective.'

This verse tells us that our prayers are powerful as long as our hearts are right with God and that prayer can change any situation that you may be going through.

So what happens when you pray:
It brings you closer to God and you can have fellowship with Him. Prayer builds you up spiritually and helps you overcome Satan.

Gives you the wisdom, revelation, and knowledge of Christ and allows you to glorify God with praise and thanksgiving.

God gives you grace, mercy, and peace and makes His presence real to you.

He brings you healing for your mind, body, and spirit and gives you strength to face your problems.

Helps you realize that He will provide for your every need and open the way to a Spirit-filled life that enables you to receive spiritual gifts.

God gives you power for ministry and helps you understand His Will for your life.

He will guide you and help you to witness to the lost and help you lead them to the lord

Prayer reminds us that Christ intercedes to God for you. **Romans 8:34**

We may be intimidated to pray at first especially if we hear others pray long elaborate prayers. Jesus' prayers were simple and to the point. But there were times He prayed all night long.

We need to pray often; not forgetting or neglecting to but at all times. Of course this does not mean that we have to be on our knees 24hrs a day. But we should be consistent in our prayer life and think about Him during the day and all the wonderful blessings He has given us. We need to thank Him for what He has done, what He is doing and what He is about to do.

Another form of prayer is to sing praises to the Lord.
Pray before each meal whether at home or in a restaurant.
We need to make time for God. He is always there when we call on Him.
Don't just pray when you have a need but pray when things are going well. Those are the prayers of thanksgiving.
When you pray, just speak to the Lord as you would to your best friend. Because that is what He wants to be to you. You do not have to speak out fancy words and phrases. Just be yourself.

Matthew 6:6 tells us to go to our room, close the door and pray. Why? Jesus is our example. He spent a lot of time by Himself in prayer. He prayed so intently that His sweat was like drops of blood (**Luke** 22:44).

You are more likely to pour out your heart to God when no one is around and listening. Whether you kneel or walk around praying makes no difference. The most important thing is just to pray. God wants you to unload your heavy burdens on Him.

The Lord's Prayer is a great example of how to pray.

Matthew 6:9 - 13 NKJV
'In this manner therefore pray;
Our Father in Heaven, hallowed be Your name,
Your kingdom come, Your will be done, on earth as it is in
Heaven.
Give us this day our daily bread.
And forgive us our debts, as we forgive our debtors.
And do not lead us not into temptation, but deliver us from the
evil one, For Yours is the kingdom and the power and the
glory forever. Amen!'

This prayer contains six petitions; three concerning the Holiness and Will of God and three concerned with our personal needs.

Here is a breakdown of this prayer verse by verse.

Our Father in Heaven:

As our Father, God loves us, cares for us, and welcomes our fellowship and intimacy. We can pray to Him any time day or night to worship Him and communicate our needs to Him.

Hallowed be Your name:

The word 'Hallowed' means Sacred, Holy, Revered, and Respected. What better names can we use for our Heavenly Father? He is our creator and deserves respect at all times. His name is Holy, and we should glorify and exalt Him. But people today use His name in a derogatory and mocking way. How this must hurt Him. It's easy to pick up the ways and speech of the world but it is so important that His name should be reverenced at all times.

Philippians 2:9 NIV
'Therefore God exalted Him (Jesus) to the highest place and gave Him the name that is above every name.'

Your kingdom come:

We should always pray for Christ's return.
The bible tells us that God will one day destroy this earth and set up a new kingdom where those who are saved will live for eternity. This may sound scary but also exciting. **Rev 21:1**
Although we wait for that day we cannot forget that God is still working here on earth. He has given His children the power to destroy the works of Satan, to save the lost, and pray over the sick. **2 Timothy 1:7**

Your Will be done on earth as it is in Heaven:

What is the Will of God?

He wants all people to believe in Jesus Christ and accept Him as their Lord and Savior. **John 6:40, 1 John 3:23**

That we should live holy and godly lives and be an example to those around us. **1 Timothy 4:12; 1 Peter 5:3**

We should give God thanks for all the seen and unseen things He does for us. **1 Thessalonians 5:18**

Although the Bible is a complete revelation of God's Will, there are always decisions we must make that are not covered by specific statements of Scripture. To know God's Will in such instances we must be in fellowship with the Lord.! **1 Corinthians 1:9**

If you are unsure about a decision you have to make it's always best to pray about it before you act. And while you are praying also ask Him to close the door if it is not His will for you to do it. There will be times that you will make a wrong decision that can be hard to live with, but God can help you get through it. So don't decide anything in haste.

<u>**Give us this day our daily bread**</u>*:*

This is the time to pray for your needs. God cares for you and will provide all your needs. **Matthew 6:25- 34,**

The Bible tells us in **Matthew 6:8** *that the Father knows what you need even before you ask.*

Philippians 4:6 *tells us not to worry or be anxious about anything.*

Isaiah 65:24 tells us that He hears our prayers and answers them while we are still talking.

What wonderful promises God gives us.

Forgive us our debts as we forgive our debtors:

It's wonderful to know that God will forgive us when we fail but it is sometimes hard for us to forgive those that have wronged us one way or another. However many times God forgives us we must also forgive those that sin against us.

Matthew 6:14 - 15 NIV
'For if you forgive other people when they sin against you, your Heavenly Father will also forgive you.
But if you do not forgive others their sins, your Father will not forgive your sins.'

We must not hold a grudge, hatred, or bitterness in our hearts but instead **'be kind and compassionate to one another forgiving each other, just as in Christ God forgave you'** *Ephesians 4:32.*

Also, read **Colossians 3:12-13**

And do not lead us into temptation, but deliver us from the evil one:

God will never lead us into temptation - that job belongs to Satan. Satan hates all those who love the Lord, and we need to be on our guard knowing that he will try to trip us up any way he can. By covering ourselves in prayer daily and totally depending on God for protection, we can have the assurance that God is watching over us. **2 Timothy 4:18, 2 Peter 2:9**

For yours is the kingdom and the power and the glory:

This part of the Lord's Prayer is not acknowledged by all versions of the Bible. But it is a very necessary part, as it is about 'WORSHIP.' God is worthy; we need to praise Him.

Psalms 113:3 NIV
'From the rising of the sun to the place where it sets, the name of the Lord is to be praised.'

Psalms 34:1 NKJV
'I will bless the Lord at all times; His praise shall continually be in my mouth.'

Finally: 'Listen'

John 10:27 NIV
'My sheep listen to My voice, I know them, and they follow Me.'

Listening is just as important as praying. Give God the chance to speak to you. You may never hear the voice of God. but He will speak to you either through thoughts, with a feeling, or a burden that He may have placed on your heart. Allow God to respond to you.

HOW SHOULD I PRAY:

1. *The first thing is to __PRAISE__ God.*
2. *Then __CONFESS__ any sin in your life.*
3. *Next is __PETITION__. Asking God to supply your needs.*
4. *Then comes __THANKSGIVING__. Thanking God for what He has already done.*
5. *The last thing is __COMMITMENT__. Committing your life to God.*

Prayer Questions

1. Does God want to answer your prayers? **Matt** 7:11 (1 book in N.T)

2. What is the prayer God recognizes from sinners? **Luke** 18: 10 – 14 (3rd book in N.T)
V13_____

3. When we pray, what must we do in order to receive an answer? **Matthew** 21:22 (1st book in N.T)

4. What assurance can we have that, when we pray we will receive an answer? **1 John** 5:14-15 (23rd book in N.T)

5. If you can get two or more people to pray and agree, what does God promise will happen? **Matthew** 18:19 – 20 (1st book in N.T)

6. How should we approach God when we pray? **Hebrews** 4:16 (19th book in N.T)

7. Will God provide for you? **Matthew** 6:25 – 34 (1st book in N.T)

8. What name did God give Jesus? **Philippians** 2:9 (11th book in NT)

9. What is the Father's Will for us? **John** 6:40 (4th book in N.T)

10. What kind of example should we set before others. **1 Timothy** 4:12 (14th book in N.T)

11. What happens when we do not forgive others? **Matthew 6:14 - 15** (1ˢᵗ book in N.T)

12. Where should the name of the Lord be praised? **Psalm 113:3** (19ᵗʰ book in N.T)

Memorize: Philippians 4:6, 1 John 5:14 - 15

My Journal

Study The Bible

The Word of God

John 1:1 *in this verse John is calling 'Jesus' the Word. When you hear others speak, their words reveal the type of person they are, the way they are living their lives, and what is important to them. When we think of Jesus as the Word it reveals the heart and mind of God.*

God gave us the Bible as a guide to use in our daily lives. It's our instruction manual. He wants us to live godly and victorious lives. He is telling us that we must read, study, and memorize His Word.

We should read the Bible daily and reflect on His Word and apply it to every area of our lives. If we do this God will give us the wisdom to live a righteous or godly life and help us to achieve His goals for our lives.

If you don't know the Word (bible) you won't know the promises and blessings available to you. It is also one of the best ways to hear from God and get to know Him.

When you pray you are talking to God and when you read His Word 'He reveals to us great and unsearchable things we do not know.'
Jeremiah 33:3

Some may say that they don't have time or they may not like to read, but there are other ways to hear the Word. Bible on CD, audiobooks, etc. are easily available from your local library and the internet.

How do we study the Bible?

The Bible is a very complex book and can be difficult to understand. It is packed with important facts and promises.

So, it is easy to get overwhelmed and when we feel like that we may put the bible away and hope that the next time we try, it will be a little easier.
Before you open the Bible pray and ask God to help you understand what you will be reading.

I like to keep a pen and notebook next to me as I study. You never know when something will jump off the page, something you hadn't seen or understood before, or something God wants to show you. We will never completely understand all we read in the bible but the more you study, the more He will reveal to you.

Think about the words that are used and how they relate to one another. If you can get in the habit of reading the bible every day it will help you get into a routine. And some of us need a routine to get things done throughout the day. There will be days that circumstances won't allow you to study so don't beat yourself up. The following day, just pick up where you left off. The more you read the easier it will get.

Psalms 119:105 *His Word will guide and direct you, and help you to live according to His will. So trust Him and live your best life.*

It might help to read over a verse or passage a few times. This will help you memorize those verses. If you have memorized a portion of the Word of God, you can gain insights into its meaning at times when a Bible is not readily available.

And it's really important to memorize God's Word as it will help you combat Satan when he tries to manipulate your thoughts and actions. It can also help when you are talking to others about the Lord. Everything we say and do must be backed up with the Word of God.

The more you read, study, and memorize the Word of God the more He will reveal to you.'

We also need to meditate on God's Word

Joshua 1:8 NIV
Keep this book of the Law (Bible) always on your lips; meditate on it day and night, so that you may be careful to do everything written in it. Then you will be prosperous and successful.'

Psalms 119:148 *tells us to meditate all night even if sleep must be missed.*

If you are troubled and cannot sleep it will sometimes help to read your Bible and meditate on God's Word. Just reading the promises He has given to us will help ease your mind and give you the peace you need to get through whatever struggles you are experiencing. Just rest in the Lord and know He is with you and working on your behalf.

We need to hide the Word in our hearts so we will not sin against God. Psalms 119:11

How will we respond to God's Word? Do we believe it and want to live by it or will we mock and turn away from it?

***Hebrews 4:12** tells us that God's Word is a powerful and sharp weapon that God will use to judge us. Whether our thoughts and motives are spiritual or worldly. It has two edges either cutting to save lives or judging us to eternal death. I pray that your response will be to believe and that you will draw closer to the Lord.*

Study Questions

1. What is the Word of God? **John 1:1** (4th book in NT)

2. What can you do to understand what you read?

3. When you read the Bible, what does it reveal? **Jeremiah 33:3** (24th book in OT)

4. How often should you meditate on the Word? **Psalms 119:148** (19th book in OT)

5. What can we gain by memorizing scripture?

6. Why do we need to hide the Word in our hearts? **Psalms 119:11** (19th book in OT)

My Journal

The Armor of God

How many times have we walked into or moved into a house that did not feel quite right? I have, and sometimes they had a feeling of eeriness about them. When I was a young Christian I had no idea what that feeling was but over the years, through teachings and study, I realized that on occasion, demons could take up residence in homes. At first, I was quite scared whenever there was talk of demons. But later I realized that the fear I felt came from Satan and I reacted exactly how he wanted me to act.

Whenever we are in the presence of evil we must use discernment, regarding the course of action we should take. There is an old saying, 'fools rush in where wise men fear to tread.' There is some truth to that saying.

There are things we must always do before facing the enemy. The most important is to bathe ourselves in prayer. Prayer has such protection in it. We should never start our day without prayer. Many times it may dictate how our day will progress, develop, etc.

There are times in my Christian walk when I come under attack. This happens more often when I am tired. Satan looks for a back door, a crack in my foundation, and patiently waits for the right moment to attack.

No soldier goes into battle without his armour or weapons.
To keep us strong against the enemy's attack, you must put on the full armour of God. This armour we are talking about is not man-made. It is the armour that God places on us to prepare us for battle.

*In **Ephesians 6:12** NKJV the bible tells us who we are fighting*

*Reading **1 Samuel 17** you will find the story of David and Goliath. It shows us how God can work in our lives if we allow Him.*

David developed a close relationship with his Heavenly Father at a young age. As a young man he watched his family's sheep. He killed a lion and a bear when they tried to take lambs from the flock, He may have been the youngest of his family, but God knew how brave he was. You see, David was significant in God's eyes.

When his country came under attack and went to war, David was asked by his father to take food to his brothers who were with King Saul. As he entered the camp he found the men being intimidated by a man named Goliath.

When King Saul heard the things that David had been saying to the men, he wanted to hear for himself, so he summoned David to come to him. David reassured the king that he was willing to face Goliath and through the power of God, he would kill him.

So the king dressed David in his own armour to prepare him for battle but when David tried to walk he found it impossible to move. David knew that the armour would not work but allowed the king the satisfaction of trying. So instead of the manmade armour, David picked up his slingshot and five small stones and faced the enemy, killing Goliath with just one of those stones. But David did not face the enemy alone, he knew that God was on his side and would help him to be victorious.

What is the giant in your life? Is it an abusive relationship, a bill collector, or maybe a drug addiction? Whatever battle you are facing, be sure to put on the full armour of God before stepping on the battlefield.

Ephesians 6:10-18 NIV
'Finally, be strong in the Lord and His mighty power.
Put on the full armour of God so that you can take your stand against the devil's schemes.'
For our struggle is not against flesh and blood, but against the rulers, against the authorities, against the powers of this dark world and against the spiritual forces of evil in the heavenly realms.
Therefore put on the full armour of God, so that when the day of evil comes, you may be able to stand your ground, and after you have done everything, to stand.
Stand firm then, with the Belt of Truth buckled around your waist, with the Breastplate of Righteousness in place,
And with your feet fitted with the readiness that comes from the Gospel of Peace.
In addition to all this, take up the Shield of Faith, with which you can extinguish all the flaming arrows of the evil one.

Take the Helmet of Salvation and the Sword of the Spirit, which is the Word of God.
And pray in the Spirit on all occasions with all kinds of prayers and requests. With this in mind, be alert and always keep on praying for all the saints.

When we become Christians, we become part of God's army and we begin a spiritual battle against all evil.

God empowers us so we can go into battle and conquer the enemy, but we do not fight the same way that the world fights 2 **Corinthians** 10:4.

Our goal should be to eliminate the control that Satan has over us.

He tries to entice us into worldly temptations that are so against the godly life that Jesus wants us to live [I Peter 2:11; Galatians 5:17;

James 1:14-15; I John 2:16].

I have listed some of the things that we are expected to do and will experience while in the battle. This list was taken from 'The Full Life Study Bible.'

In their warfare of faith Christians are called on to endure hardships like:

1. Good soldiers of Christ [2 **Timothy** 2:3],
2. Suffer for the gospel [**Matthew** 5:10 – 12; **Romans** 8:17; 2 **Corinthians** 11:23; 2 **Timothy** 1:8],
3. Fight the good fight of faith [1 **Timothy** 6:12; 2 **Timothy** 4:7],
4. Wage war [2 **Corinthians** 10:3],
5. Persevere [**Ephesians** 6:18],
6. Conquer [**Romans** 8:37],
7. Be victorious [1 **Corinthians** 15:57];
8. Triumph [2 **Corinthians** 2:14],
9. Defend the gospel [**Philippians** 1:16],
10. Contend for the faith [**Philippians** 1:27; **Jude** 3],
11. Not be frightened by opponents [**Philippians** 1:28],

12. Put on the full armor of God, stand firm [*Ephesians 6:14*],

13. Destroy Satan's strongholds [*2 Corinthians 10:4*],

14. Take captive every thought [*2 Corinthians 10:5*],

15. Become powerful in battle [*Hebrews 11:34*].'

God gave us six pieces of armour to protect us from our enemy.

The Belt Of Truth

The soldiers of the era when this scripture was written wore a leather belt around their waist that would keep the rest of their armour in place. Today, our spiritual belt of truth is the center of our Christian beliefs. We must believe and have a spiritual knowledge of the truth.

What is the truth? We must believe that Jesus died to free us from sin. That He rose from the dead and is now living in Heaven with God the Father. That He hears our prayers and intercedes on our behalf to the Father.

Jesus tells us in: **John 8:32 'Then you will know the truth and the truth will set you free.'**

Jesus is truth, and through our belief in Him, He will set us free from the enemy's clutches.

There would not be any reason to go into a battle if you did not believe in the reason to fight. There is always a 'cause' for those who go into battle. Our 'cause' as Christians is to fight against what the enemy is trying to do to us, as individuals, our families, and our country. We must continue to stand up for that truth in our daily walk with God, knowing that He walks beside us and strengthens us every step of the way.

Breastplate Of Righteousness

The breastplate of righteousness represents a holy and moral character. We as Christians should display this kind of character in our everyday lives.

The breastplate protects the heart from injury. We know that Satan wants to attack the heart. He knows our weaknesses and will try to tempt us into doing things that are the opposite of our moral character.

John 10:10 NIV
'The thief [Satan] comes only to steal, kill, and destroy.'

We must guard our hearts at all costs and not compromise our faith and the things that we know are right. It may seem easier to give in to the enemy rather than to make a stand when he attacks. He tries to scare us and intimidate us.
But we must continue to persevere through those trials as this is the time that God strengthens and builds character in us. We are then able to withstand everything that the enemy puts in our way. **Romans 5: 3-4**

Gospel Of Peace

As we have read in **Ephesians** 6:15 we should make ourselves ready for battle by putting on the shoes of readiness. These shoes give us a sense of eagerness that we are ready to advance against Satan's army. And through all this, God's peace comes upon us and strengthens us to continue the fight. **Psalm 60:12; John 14:27**

I have been in many battles in my spiritual walk, and the sense of peace that God gives me always amazes me, We must learn to lean and trust in Him through those bad times so we can be victorious over our enemy.

1 John 5:4-5 NIV
'For everyone born of God overcomes the world. This is the victory that has overcome the world, even our faith.
Who is it that overcomes the world? Only the one who believes that Jesus is the Son of God.'

Shield Of Faith

The Bible tells us that our enemy shoots his fiery darts at us hoping to wound us. The shield of faith must protect us from those fiery darts. A soldier's shield would have been large enough to cover his body against the arrows and swords of his enemy and also helped to protect the rest of his armor.

In the book 'Handbook for Spiritual Warfare, Revised' by Dr Ed Murphy, it states that: 'The round shield of the early [Roman] legionnaires had long since been elongated [the scutum], two-thirds covered his body and one-third covered his comrade to the left. This brilliant innovation encouraged tight ranks, since each fighter was in part dependent on his neighbor for protection.'

The shield of faith is our belief in God and all His promises. Your shield of faith must be large enough to withstand every assault that Satan tries to inflict on you. He will try to tempt you to think wrong thoughts, persecute you in your body, finances, relationships, and fill you with doubt and despair. He will send false teachers to try to lead you away from God.

But a strong faith in God will help you stay strong and resist everything that the enemy is trying to do to you. Without it, Satan can put all kinds of doubt in our minds and before we know it we are ready to give up and give in. But don't let that happen, don't listen to the lies of the enemy. The bible also tells us that the battle has already been won; we just need to stand our ground.

How is your faith today? Is it great enough to protect you from the enemy? Is it strong enough to help a friend who is lacking faith in their life? Why not give all your problems, decisions and even your life, over to God today and let Him work things out for you. **1 Peter 5: 7 - 8**

<u>Helmet Of Salvation</u>

If you have accepted Jesus as your savior, there may have been times when you have doubted that salvation. When we make a mistake or a wrong choice we may think that God cannot forgive us.
That is Satan's strategy. He will attack our minds and fill us with every negative thought.
It is important to turn off that kind of thinking as soon as you realize who is prompting those thoughts.
We must realize that positive, loving, and comforting thoughts come from God. Negative thoughts that are full of fear and condemnation come from Satan.

It is so important that we become alert to our every thought. If your thoughts are coming from the enemy, you have the power to change those thoughts. **Phil 4:8**

SWORD OF THE SPIRIT

This last piece of armour is the sword of the spirit. It is the Word of God. This sword is used to attack as well as defend us against the enemy.

Satan will try everything possible to break your confidence in God's Word. But we must always keep in mind that His Word is true.
The Word of God is an awesome, powerful tool that we can use to defeat <u>all</u> the power of the enemy.

How do we use this tool?
By memorizing scripture, and keeping it hidden in our hearts and minds. I cannot emphasize enough how important it is to do this.

As disciples of Jesus, we have authority over our enemy to drive out evil spirits and to heal the sick. **Matthew 10:1**

When Satan comes around and tries to tempt you, you can resist him just like Jesus did, by speaking out the Word of God.

Matthew 4:4, 7, 10 NIV
'Jesus answered, 'It is written...'

Tell Satan that Jesus gave you authority over him and that he must leave in the name of Jesus.

James 4:7 NIV
'Submit yourselves then, to God. Resist the devil and he will flee from you.

As we are living in the last days, it is so important that we wear the armour of God daily to keep us strong for the battles we will face in the future.

There have been many times in the last few years that the attacks from Satan have been so great that spiritual warfare was the only thing I could do.
I would go into my study and walk the floor, crying out to God and rebuking the enemy.
I had determined in my mind that I was not going to let Satan win. This was the beginning of my victory.

My circumstances may not have changed but God was changing me. He was helping me deal with my situation.

With every battle I faced, God continued to strengthen me. I realized God had made me into a fighter. This was something I had never been before.

Whatever area of your life Satan is attacking you in; whether it is family, finances, health, etc. know that you can be victorious over it. You may not see changes overnight, but God is faithful and will bring you through.

I think **1 Corinthians 16:13** *shows us how our attitude should be toward spiritual warfare.*

I found this prayer many years ago. It covers every area of our lives. I encourage you to read it every day.

Heavenly Father, I humble myself in worship before you. To your Holy name be glory, honor, and praise forever! You are worthy of my adoration, devotion, and thanksgiving. I commit myself to love You with all my heart, mind, soul, and strength. Here is my body as a living sacrifice, consecrated to You and made holy as a temple of the Holy Spirit. I give myself to You completely and without holding anything back.

By faith, I claim the blood of our Lord Jesus Christ around and within me. I give myself to abide and remain in Christ during this day. In union with Christ, I take my stand against all efforts of Satan and his demons to hinder me in this time of prayer. I address myself only to the God and Father of our Lord Jesus Christ and reject any involvement of Satan in this prayer.

Satan, I command you in the all - powerful name of the Lord Jesus Christ, to leave my presence, with all your demons, and go to the place where Jesus Christ sends you. I bring His blood between us and around me as a shield. In the name of the Lord Jesus Christ, I order you not to approach me in any way except by the Heavenly Father's permission.

Righteous Father, by faith and in obedience to Your command, I put off the old self which is being corrupted by its deceitful desires and put on the new self, created to be like God in true righteousness and holiness. I resist all the forces of darkness that stimulate the desires of my sinful nature and claim the appearance of the Son of God to destroy the devil's work in my life. By the power and authority of our Lord Jesus Christ, I retake any ground given to the devil and release its full control to the Holy Spirit.

I bring all this power to bear against Satan, his forces of evil, and his strategies against me. Heavenly Father, with the divine power of weapons of righteousness that You give in Christ, I tear down Satan's strongholds in my life and in the lives of those I love. I destroy every argument and excuse for not knowing the triune God better and better. I reject the ideas and phrases that make sin attractive and plausible, by faith, I claim the mind of Christ. I take captive every thought to make it obedient to Christ. With sound judgment, I refuse to take up an offense for those who disobey Your will as revealed in Your written Word or to defend them in any way. I ask for insight to restore gently someone caught in a sin. I demolish the plans of Satan formed against me today. I smash the plans of Satan against my heart and carefully guard my affections. I break the stronghold of Satan against my emotions. I release anxiety, bitterness, anger, loneliness, and lust, replacing them with the peace of God that transcends all understanding. I smash the strongholds of Satan against my mind and meditate on Your Word day and night. I obliterate the strongholds of Satan formed against my will and choose now to trust and obey the Lord Jesus Christ. I crush the strongholds formed against my spirit and set my path to live constantly and continuously in the fullness of the Holy Spirit.

I shatter the strongholds of Satan formed against my body and invite the Holy Spirit to fill my body and use its parts today for the glory of Jesus Christ. I splinter the strongholds of the devil against my soul and yield the depths of my personality into Your care. I burst the strongholds of the enemy against any and every part of myself and bring my deepest desires to You for satisfaction.

In obedience to the command in Your Word, I commit myself to be strong in the Lord and His mighty power. Thank You for the full armor of God that You provide. Right now I put on the belt of truth, the breastplate of righteousness, and the boots of readiness that comes from the gospel of peace. I hold up the shield of faith that extinguishes all the flaming arrows of the evil one. I put on the helmet of salvation; I grasp the sword of the spirit, which is the Word of God. Train me to use it with supernatural ability. Stimulate me to pray on all occasions and with all kinds of prayers and requests.

Thank you, Lord Jesus, for loving me and laying down Your life for me. Open my eyes today for the opportunities to love others and to lay down my life for them. Grant me opportunities to use the spiritual gifts You have given me in a spirit of humility, joy, and service. Help me to take my focus off myself and to fix my eyes on Jesus Christ and on those You want me to love and serve. I enter this day with thanksgiving and praise. Open my eyes to what You are doing, Holy Father, and allow me to be used by the Holy Spirit as a part of it. I pray in the confidence of the wonderful name of our Lord Jesus Christ who is able to keep me from falling and to present me before Your glorious presence without fault and with great joy.

Amen!

Author Unknown

Armour of God Questions

1. What are the 6 pieces of armour we are supposed to wear? **Ephesians 6:13 - 18** (10th book in N.T)

2. What does Satan want to do to us? **John 10:10** (4th book in NT)
3. Who are our enemies? **Ephesians 6:12** (10th book in N.T)

4. Who overcomes the world? **1 John 5:4 – 5** (4th book in NT)

5. What are we to think of when Satan tries to manipulate our minds? **Philippians 4:8** (11th boon in N.T)

6. What must we do to make Satan leave us alone? **James 4:7** (20th book in (N.T)

7. What does God give us when He tells us not to be afraid? **John 14:27** (4th book in NT)

8. Since Satan is trying his best to draw us away from God what are we supposed to do? **1Peter 5:8** (21st book in N.T)

9. When we know the truth what will it do for us? **John 8:32** (4th book in N.T)

My Journal

Baptism in the Holy Spirit

The Baptism in the Holy Spirit is a controversial subject in many churches. We know we receive the Holy Spirit when we accept Christ as our Savior, but being filled with the Spirit goes much further than that. So I will attempt to write about the 3rd part of the Trinity. But what is the Trinity? It is made up of the Father, Son, and Holy Spirit.

*We know that God created the heavens and the earth **Genesis 1:1**. Then the next verse says the Spirit of God hovered over the waters.*
***John 1:1-2** tells us 'In the beginning was the Word (Jesus), and the Word (Jesus) was with God and the Word (Jesus) was God, the same was in the beginning with God*

*Putting these all together we then read **Gen 1:26** 'Let US make man in our image.' So we can see that the Father, Jesus, and the Holy Spirit are all one God. The Holy Spirit is as much a person as the Father and the Son.*

God the Father created us.
God the Son came to die for us.
God the Holy Spirit is here to lead us into eternity.

*As we are learning about God we should have a hunger to get to know Him and we should have the desire to obey Him. Because we are human it is impossible for us to live a perfect, sinless life. Only Jesus was able to live that sinless life because He is the Son of God. Jesus asked His Father to send another helper/advocate, the Holy Spirit to us to help us **John 14:16**, guide us and convict us when we do wrong things.*
*But being filled with the baptism of the Holy Spirit goes beyond all of this. The Holy Spirit brings boldness **Acts 4:31**, and wisdom **Acts 6:10**; **Ephesians 1:17**; **Colossians 1:9** to the believer. He teaches us what to say and do in certain situations **Luke 12:12**. He brings us power **Acts 1:8**, guidance, **John 16:13**, and strength **1 Timothy 1:12** to do the things that God wants us to do. **Romans 8:26 - 27** He intercedes our prayers to God.*

***Acts 2:38** tells us that we must repent before we can be filled with the baptism of the Holy Spirit. It is the next step in the Christian life process.*

Allow people to counsel and pray for you. When that hungry desire to be filled with the Spirit consumes you, and you are ready to let God control your life, that's when it will happen.

When John the Baptist preached to the people about repentance and being baptized he says in **Luke 3:16** *'I baptize you with water. But one who is more powerful than I will come, the straps of whose sandals I am not worthy to untie. He will baptize you with the Holy Spirit and fire.'*

Many verses in the Bible mention Jesus speaking to His disciples (His followers) about the Holy Spirit. When we accept Jesus as our Savior we also become His disciples and everything He promised His disciples then is a promise for us today.

Luke 24:49 *Jesus told them that His Father promised to send the Holy Spirit and that it was a gift God was sending to them* **Acts 2:38**

The Baptism of the Holy Spirit is not given to you so you can be powerful and impressive. It is given, so you will have the boldness to be a witness to the lost.

Before Peter received the Holy Spirit he was just like us. In **Matthew 26:33 – 35** *Peter thought was strong enough to face anything, and that he was in control of his life. But in* **Matthew 26:69 – 75** *we find him denying the Lord and running away.*

In **Acts 2:14 – 41** *after Peter has been filled with the Baptism of the Holy Spirit, we find him preaching the Gospel to thousands of people. About three thousand people were saved that day. He has a boldness about him now and can do the work that God wants him to do.*

When you receive this supernatural gift, the evidence will be speaking in tongues. Which means you will speak words or utter sounds you do not understand. Some speak languages they never learned or even a language unknown to men.

You are not seeking tongues, you are seeking God. If you have not experienced tongues you are not Spirit-filled. You are saved, the Spirit is in you but there is more for you to seek.

So, after being filled with the Holy Spirit how can you use this spiritual language?

Praying for someone:
You may not always know what that person is praying for, or what their particular need is but God does. Sometimes, while you are praying for that person God will reveal to you their need and you can pray specifically for that need. But if God does not reveal it to you and the person does not tell you then always pray that God's will be done in their lives and situations.

To edify yourself in the Spirit:
We all get discouraged at times so praying in tongues can build up our faith.

To give a message in tongues:
At church, we may hear someone give a message in tongues, and then another person will interpret that message. When we hear the interpretation of that message it can be for a specific person or the church itself. God has ways to encourage us individually and corporately. If you are willing, the Holy Spirit will use you [work through you] to accomplish the things He wants to be done.
Read **1 Corinthians** 12:1 - 11. The Gifts of the Spirit.

How often should we pray in the Spirit?
Everyday! When you start your prayers it will be in your regular language. But as you pray the more intense prayers, then you can pray in tongues. It's not something you can turn on and off. Sometimes during praise and worship, I get such a feeling rising inside me that I have to quit singing and start speaking in tongues and praising God.

Remember, when you pray in your regular language you know that God hears your prayers but so does Satan. When you talk to God in your Heavenly language God knows what you are saying but Satan cannot interpret.

In **Ephesians** 1:13 - 14 we see that we are marked with God's seal, the promised Holy Spirit. And God marks us as His own: **2 Corinthians** 1:22. The Spirit delivers us from the power of sin: **Romans** 8:1 - 17

He gives us a consciousness of God as our Father: **Romans 8:15;** *Galatians 4:6*

And He fills us with power to witness for Him: **Acts 1:8**

In the book of Ephesians: The Holy Spirit:

1. *Is the mark or seal of God's ownership [1:13]*
2. *Is the first installment of the believer's inheritance [1:14]*
3. *Is the Spirit of wisdom and revelation [1:17]*
4. *Helps the believer when he or she draws near to God [2:18]*
5. *Builds the body of believers into a holy temple [2:21 - 22]*
6. *Reveals the mystery of Christ [3:4 - 5]*
7. *Strengthens the believer with power in the inner being [3:16]*
8. *Motivates unity in the Christian faith in full Christlikeness [4:3, 13 - 14]*
9. *Grieves when there is sin in the life of the believer [4:30]*
10. *Desires to repeatedly fill and empower the believer [5:18]*
11. *Helps in prayer and spiritual warfare [6:18]*

In this age the Holy Spirit is given to believers as a down payment of what we are going to have in greater fullness in the future.
His presence and work in our lives is a pledge of our inheritance.
Romans 8:23;
2 Corinthians 1:22; 5:5

Psalms 139:7 *David asks God 'where can I go from Your Spirit or where can I flee from Your presence?*

Holy Spirit Questions

1. What was the first promise John gave the world regarding receiving the Baptism of the Holy Spirit? **Luke 3:16** (3rd book in N.T)

2. What must we do before we can receive the Holy Spirit? **Acts 2:38** (5th book in N.T)

3. Because Jesus felt it was so important that we receive the Holy Spirit, what did He say He would do about it? **John 14:16** (4th book in N.T).

4. What is the primary purpose of being filled with the Holy Spirit? **Acts 1:8** (5th book in N.T)

5. How do we know the Baptism of the Holy Spirit is a separate experience from salvation? **Acts 8:14 - 16** (5th book in N.T)

Verse 14:

Verse 15_____

Verse 16

6. What does the Holy Spirit give us to help us minister to others? **Ephesians 1:17** (10th book in N.T)

7. What is the initial outward evidence that a person has received the Baptism in the Holy Spirit? **Acts 2:4** (5th book in N.T)

8. How does speaking in tongues help your prayer life? **Romans 8:26 - 27** (6th book in N.T)

9. Why is the Holy Spirit so important to my life:

   John 16:13 (4Th book in N.T)

   Acts 9:31 (5th book in N.T)

10. How do we know we belong to God? **Ephesians** 1:13 – 14 (10th book in N.T) **2 Corinthians** 1:22 (8th book in N.T)

Memorize: **Acts** 2:39, **Acts** 1:8

My Journal

Beauty Of A Woman

The beauty of a woman is not in the clothes she wears,
The figure she carries, or the way she combs her hair.

The beauty of a woman must be seen from her eyes,
Because that is the doorway to her heart,
The place where love resides.

The beauty of a woman is not a facial mole,
But true beauty in a woman is reflected in her soul.

It is in the caring that she lovingly gives, the passion that she shows.
The beauty of a woman with time only grows

Author Unknown

You are beautiful and you are loved!!

'Beauty is in the eye of the beholder so the saying goes. When we look into a mirror what do we see? Most of the time we don't like that image looking back at us. Instead of seeing the beauty, we focus on the flaws we think we have. Maybe it's a blemish that we think everyone can see or those wrinkles that are beginning to show. Outward appearance is important to us, we all want to feel pretty and attractive. When we feel good our confidence shows it. We'll stand a little straighter and put on our special smile and we walk with determination.

But what does God see when He looks at you? He sees beauty. You were made in His image; He created and loves you and He desires to have a relationship with you. **Psalms 100:5; Romans 5:8; 1 John 3:1**

This love that He has for you is immeasurable, our minds cannot comprehend that kind of love.

Regardless of the life you lived before giving your heart to God, you need to remember that He loves you and doesn't condemn you. All those sins you did in the past are now nailed to the cross. He wants to help you stay strong no matter what life throws at you, but it takes baby steps, so don't think it will happen overnight

Titus 2:11 – 12 NIV
*'For the grace of God has appeared that offers salvation to all people.
It teaches us to say 'No' to ungodliness and worldly passions and to live self-controlled, upright, and godly lives in this present age.'*

We should be careful not to provoke impure thoughts and immoral desires in others that can cause them to sin. **Matthew 5:28**

But we do need to be aware of our lifestyle, our dress, and our speech as we learn how to become children of God.

1 Peter 3:3-4 NIV
*'Your beauty should not come from outward adornments, such as elaborate hairstyles and the wearing of gold jewelry or fine clothes.
Rather it should be that of your inner self, the unfading beauty of a gentle and quiet spirit, which is of great worth in God's sight.'*

1 Timothy 2:9-10 NIV
*'I also want women to dress modestly, with decency and propriety, adorning themselves not with elaborate hairstyles or gold and pearls or expensive clothes.
But with good deeds, appropriate for women who profess to worship God.'*

These scriptures are not saying that you cannot wear fine clothes, jewelry, and such. The world may look on them as a necessary tool to attract attention.
But we need to be aware of what we wear. God wants us to dress modestly. Most of the women today dress to draw attention to themselves. But that is not what God expects of us, these are not the things that make you beautiful.

In **1 Timothy 2:9** it talks about Decency, Modestly, Propriety
These are the definitions of them:

Decency - *respectability*
Modesty - *in a way that shows regard for decency in behavior, speech, and dress*
Propriety - *standards of good and proper behavior and manners*

Our speech is also important. We should not talk as the world talks using bad language and gossiping. **Ephesians 4:29**

What kind of words do you speak? Are they words full of offensive language, are they hateful and malicious, or are they words of kindness and encouragement?

It's amazing how we can pour the bad into a person without realizing it by just being unaware or insensitive to their feelings.

In **Ephesians 4:32** and **Colossians 3:12** God tells us we should be kind, compassionate and forgiving, humble, gentle, and patient.

These are the things God wants us to develop, this inner beauty that will last for the rest of your life. It reflects who we are, the way we think, and the way we treat others. The love we have for our Heavenly Father, showing love and compassion towards others and speaking in love when arguments arise, all of these are important.

So when others look at you I hope they can see that inner beauty. When they look in your eyes that they can see Jesus and they can tell by your lifestyle and your speech that you love the Lord.

1 John 4:19 *NKJV*
'We love Him because He first loved us.'

Because He loves us He wants us to live life to the full. As women, our thoughts eventually go toward dating and getting married.
There are issues we need to think about before starting on this journey, so let's begin.

And it all starts with choices.

God allows us to make our own choices in life. The choice to accept Him as your Lord and Savior. The choice to live a godly life regardless of what the world says. The choice to pick your friends [hopefully they will *have good moral principles] and in this country the choice to marry whomever we choose.*

We also choose how we present ourselves to the world. If you profess to be a Christian then you're representing God. When people look at you they should see that you are separate from the world and your acts and deeds should reflect that.

What are you looking for in a spouse? Are you looking by using your emotions only?
Do you feel desperate? Do you feel that life is passing you by? Are you willing to accept the first proposal that comes your way even though you are not really in love with this man?

Are you looking at the physical attraction only or the amount of wealth that person has? This is not the way to choose a mate. We will get old one day and our physical appearance will change. You may lose your job, money, etc. and you may have to struggle financially for a while. If these are the values you are basing a marriage on you can expect to have problems, maybe more than you can bear.

Are any of you considering God? Are you asking Him who your mate should be?
This is your starting point. Ask God to bring into your life the person that He has chosen for you.

Love is a very strong emotion, and some people play on this emotion. They try to play mind games with you, trying to get you to do things you are not comfortable doing.

God expects us to stay sexually pure until we get married. If the person you are dating wants to be sexually active and they are not willing to wait until marriage, that shows a lack of respect for you, and they are only thinking of themselves.
You need to ask yourself, 'after marriage will this person expect me to change my convictions and do things I know are not right.'

Some may make you feel afraid that this is your last chance at love. That you must be willing to do whatever they want you to do so you will not be left alone. Their goal is to manipulate and control you.

It is easy for us to continually fall into the same situation time and again. We may look at people and wonder why that keeps happening. It could be the woman either feels some kind of comfort level with a particular type of man or Satan has her so convinced that that's the only type that would care for her.
How easily we are deceived.

You need to run away from this type of person. They are not sent from God because God loves you and never wants to hurt you. He will give you the strength to walk away. You will be much happier being alone than being with someone like that.

If you have been alone for a while, you may be anticipating dating again. What a scary thought. So where does one begin?

You should first examine your past relationships. Were they healthy relationships where you could be yourself or were you caught in a web where you could do nothing for yourself, you were dominated, etc.?

Was your partner a Christian in the right sense of the word, or in name only?
Did you ask God if this was the person He had picked for you?
Most of the time the answer to that question will be 'no.' When we enter relationships, we do not think to ask God questions, usually through ignorance, not realizing how important it is to talk to Him about everything that is happening in your life and every decision you need to make.

The next thing to consider is what you want and expect in a man. Make a list just as you would when setting goals for your life. Why? Because that is exactly what you are doing. Do not settle for less than what you know God wants for you.

One very important item on your list should be a 'Christian' man, one who loves God and shows it by the way he lives his life.

The Bible tells us in **2 Corinthians 6:14-15** that we should be careful who we let into our lives. Believers and unbelievers have little in common.

Before becoming involved in another relationship you need to consider your relationship with God. You will not become completely whole until you have a strong foundation under you. That foundation must be built on Christ.

If you have been sexually active in the past or even had an affair with a married man or someone other than your spouse, don't think all is lost. Our God is a loving and forgiving God. All you have to do is ask for forgiveness and make every effort not to do it again.
One of the hardest things to do is to forgive yourself. Satan knows this and he will always try to bring these thoughts back into your mind, to make you feel unworthy and even cause you to become depressed.

But remember this, Jesus died so your sins could be forgiven. He washed you with His blood and you became a new person, and He no longer sees your sins. So now is the time to forgive yourself. Every time Satan tries to bring your past back into your mind, tell him he must leave in the name of Jesus. And when you say, 'In The Name Of Jesus,' Satan has to leave.

Communication is another area that is very important in any relationship. Before you get married, learn to communicate with your partner. Talk about one another's past lives.
When you are open and honest about your past you will be stopping Satan from trying to bring these things back up, he will not be able to taunt you with your past or intimidate you to be afraid of anything your partner could find out about you. There should be no surprises from your past.
Remember that anything that is discussed during this time is said in confidence and should not be brought up whenever there is an argument.

Loneliness can be devastating to a person who does not know the Lord. They are just fumbling around in the dark trying to find their way out. But, if you know the Lord and have a personal relationship with Him, He will lead and guide you into places you never imagined. He will give you great joy and peace that words cannot explain. He will put people in your life to help you through rough times. He is even willing to become your husband for as long as you need Him to.

Isaiah 54:5 NIV
"For your Maker is your husband – the Lord Almighty is His name – the Holy One of Israel is your Redeemer. He is called the God of all the earth.'

God wants only the best for you, so you must learn to hear His voice. He will guide and direct you and help you through each day to become the awesome woman that He created, a woman full of purpose, ready to walk into her destiny. Honor God in everything you do, and He will bless you.

Beauty Review

1. What is inner beauty? **1 Peter 3:3-4** *(21st book in N.T)*

___

2. What do we need to develop this inner beauty?

___

3. What is the definition of Decency, Modesty, and Propriety?

___

4. What does these scriptures say about love? **John 15:9;** *(4th book in N.T)* **1 John 3:1; 4:19** *(23rd book in N.T)*

___

5. Make a list of the qualities you are looking for in a mate.

___

6. What kind of choices have you made in the past?

___

7. Is it important to find a Christian man? **2 Corinthians 6:14 – 15** *(8th book in N.T)*

___

   Why?--

8. Can God forgive all my sins? **Romans 3:23, 10:13;** *(6th book in N.T)* **1 John 1:9** *(23rd book in N.T)*

___

9. Will God remember my sins? **Romans 6:14;** *(6th book in N.T)* **Hebrews 8:12** *(19th book in N.T)*

___

10. Are you ready to allow God to help you with your decisions?

My Journal

The Christian Marriage

God created man first then He created the woman to be his helpmate. The term helpmate in no way belittles women or puts women in an inferior position to men. God created both men and women in His image to work together for His glory. We are all equal in God's eyes.

Galatians 3:28 NIV
'There is neither Jew nor Gentile, neither slave nor free, nor is there male and female, for you are all one in Christ Jesus,'

Marriage between a man and woman is ordained by God and is to be honored at all times.
From the very beginning, God speaks about this special relationship. If you are a Christian and marry a Christian God must be included in your marriage. It will certainly help when a problem arises.
Praying together as husband and wife can bring such a bond between you and will certainly strengthen your relationship. The Bible says:

Matthew 18:20 NKJV
'For where two or three are gathered together in My name, I am there in the midst of them.'

What a wonderful promise. It should give us a sense of peace knowing He cares enough for us and is willing to help us in any situation.

God is a God of order, and He has revealed to us how to live in harmony with one another, especially a husband and wife. It may not be easy, but it is so worth the effort. He desires Christians to marry Christians. The Bible tells us in:

2 Corinthians 6:14-15 NIV
'Do not be yoked together with unbelievers. For what do righteousness and wickedness have in common? Or what fellowship can light have with darkness?
What harmony is there between Christ and Belial (Satan)? Or what does a believer have in common with an unbeliever?

2 Corinthians 6:17 'Therefore, come out from them and be separate.'

What does this mean? It simply means we should not marry anyone who is not saved, living a godly life, and living up to the standards that God requires.

Marriage can be complicated, so it helps when you have things in common with one another, especially when you share the same beliefs. If you are considering marrying an unbeliever you may have a lot of challenges ahead of you.
Now I'm not saying that this type of marriage will fail, but your problems may greatly increase. As long as you stay strong in the Lord, the power of prayer can change any situation as it says in:
James 5:16 'The prayer of a righteous person is powerful and effective.'

Husbands and wives should never take each other for granted. They need to include each other in every area of their lives and find little things to say and do to each other to show their love towards their mate. Communication is so important. Don't assume your partner knows what you are thinking, more than likely they will have no clue and that can only bring problems. Be upfront and honest and explain clearly what you are trying to say.

Like every other area of our lives, God shows us how to live according to His will. He wants us to be happy [joy], and fruitful. **Genesis 1:28, 2:18**

As women, we were created to be loving companions to our husbands. So we tell ourselves 'OK we can do this but then we read the next scripture and we grind to a halt.

Ephesians 5:23 - 24 NIV
'For the husband is the head of the wife as Christ is head of the church, His body, of which He is the Savior.
Now as the church submits to
Christ, so also wives should submit to their husbands in everything.'

'There is no way I will submit to a man.'
I think all women feel this way at least once in their lives but there is so much more to be said about this if we just continue to find out what God is really telling us.

Here are the instructions that God has placed on the husband, and how He expects the husband to take care of his wife and children.

Ephesians 5:25 NIV
'Husbands, love your wives, just as Christ loved the church and gave Himself up for her.'

This verse shows us how much Christ loves us. He willingly laid down His life for us. Husbands should also love their wives in such a way that they would willingly sacrifice for her.

He should provide for his family's spiritual and domestic needs:
1 Timothy 5:8

Love, honor, understand, appreciate, and be thoughtful: **Colossians 3:19,** 1 Peter 3:7

Be faithful, not to commit adultery: **Matthew 5:27-28**
This scripture is not only talking about the husband looking lustfully at a woman but the same is said for the wife.

He must not abuse his wife: **Colossians 3:19.** As this could affect his relationship with God **1 Peter 3:7**

Titus 2:2 also gives instructions to the husband. They are to:
'Teach the older men to be temperate (agreeable), worthy of respect, self-controlled (disciplined) and sound in faith (confidence), in love, in endurance (patience.)'

1 Peter 3:7 Both men and women have equal worth before God. The husband should be gentle, know her needs and respond to them sympathetically.
They should be considerate and understanding. They should treat their wives with love, respect, and praise and live in harmony with them.

In the Jeremiah Study Bible, it lays it out very clearly.
'A husband who fails to properly love his wife makes it very difficult for her to submit to him. When a wife does not submit to her husband with respect, she makes it difficult for him to love her.'

You can see from this passage that love and respect for each other go hand in hand. If we can stay within the perimeters of our roles as husbands and wives we can have a healthy, loving marriage.

So now we come to the instructions the Lord has given to the wife.

The home, husband, and children should be at the center of a Christian wife/mother's world. When she does this she is honoring God.

She should be willing to submit to her husband: **Ephesians 5:22**

Love and respect him: **Titus 2:4; Ephesians 5:33**

Be a loving companion and helper: **Genesis 2:18; Titus 2:4-5**

Self-controlled and pure: **Titus 2:5 1 Peter 3:2**

Develop a gentle and quiet spirit: **1 Peter 3:4**

Be a good mother: **Titus 2:4**

Help to train the children to live a Godly life **Deuteronomy 6:7; 1 Timothy 5:10**

Be a good homemaker: 1 Timothy 5:14; Titus 2:5

Provide hospitality **1 Timothy 5:10**

Care for elderly parents **1 Timothy 5:8**

***Titus 2:3-5** also gives instructions to the wife*
'Likewise, teach the older women to be reverent in the way they live, not to be slanderers, or addicted to much wine, but to teach what is good, Then they can urge the young women to love their husbands and children.'
To be self-controlled and pure, to be busy at home, to be kind, and to be subject to their husband's, so that no one malign the Word of God.'

We teach others by example, so we need to be careful how we live according to God's standards. Are you respectful to everyone you meet? Are you a gossip or a slanderer? Do you show love for your family in front of others? Are you willing to teach young women how to develop that gentle spirit, and how to love their husbands? Allow God to use you. He will send women to you so you can minister to them. You can help them make the changes they need to make, then, in turn, they can minister to others.

Even though you have a great marriage there will be occasions where you'll not always agree with your spouse. It is very easy to get upset if things don't go our way. Be careful what you say because when we get angry a lot of the time we'll blurt out things that are hurtful and when this happens you cannot take those words back. Always apologize, but just saying you're sorry doesn't help the pain you have caused. Now you need to show your spouse that you love and respect them. **Ephesians 4:26**

I cannot finish this chapter without the wise words of Solomon concerning the Virtuous Wife. You will find this in **Proverbs 31:10-31**

The verses are in dark print, and the opposite of these verses are in normal print

The Opposite Of The Proverbs 31 Woman
BY JESS CONNELL

v10 *'Who can find a virtuous woman? For her price is far above rubies.'*

> A terrible wife is a dime a dozen. She is common - easily found.

v11 *'The heart of her husband safely trust in her, so he will have no lack of gain'*

> Her husband feels tense; his heart is never fully at rest around her. She blows through his resources and squanders his contributions. There's never anything left over, to invest or give. The tight finances point to a larger reality; he can't trust her.

v12 *'She does him good and not evil all the days of his life.'*

> She spends more time and energy tearing him down than building him up. Every day of her whole life is spent making him worse off.

v13 *'She seeks wool and flax, and willingly works with her hands.'*

> She sits around, aimlessly waiting for opportunities. Her hands are idle because nothing magically comes her way on its own.

v14 *'She is like the merchants' ships; she brings her food from afar.'*

> She does the bare minimum necessary to contribute to the nourishment and care of her family and sometimes, not even that! She can't be expected to go to great lengths to bless her household.

v15 *'She rises also while it is yet night, and provide food for her household and a portion for her maidens.'*

> She sleeps in, and uses her time poorly. Her household often gets to mealtime without anything planned or prepared.

v16 *'She considers a field and buys it: with the fruit of her hands she plants a vineyard.'*

She buys things on a whim – spending money on possessions rather than purposeful, long-range investments.

v17 'She girds her loins with strength, and strengthens her arms.'

She's weak-willed and weak-bodied, and thus, unwilling and unable to do things God has put on her plate.

v18 'She perceives that her merchandise is good: her lamp does not go out by night.'

Her efforts are spent unprofitably on things that don't bring fruit. If she's up late, she's doing impracticable, useless things or spending her free time as 'me time.'

v19 'She stretches her hand to the distaff, and her hands hold the spindle.'

Her skills are few if any, and what she does is careless and done poorly.

v20 'She extends her hand to the poor; yes, she reaches out her hands to the needy.'

She can't afford to be generous. The money's all gone because she spent it on other things. Her heart and hands are turned inward. Whatever her words say, the result of her actions and inaction reveal that her desires eclipse the needs of others in her heart.

v21 'She is not afraid of snow for her household: for all her household are clothed with scarlet.'

The thought of tragedy or difficulty makes her anxious and fearful because she hasn't properly prepared her home, her family, and herself for these possibilities.

v22 'She makes tapestry for herself, her clothing is fine linen and purple.'

She doesn't actively put her mind and creativity to work on improving the basic everyday things in her home.

v23 'Her husband is known in the gates when he sits among the elders of the land.'

Her husband is ridiculed and thought ill in their community because of how poorly she's talked about him. Others don't respect him because his wife doesn't either.

v24 'She makes linen garments and sells it; and supplies sashes for the merchant.

She spends her time and energy aimlessly and fruitlessly. She puts money in the pockets of the merchants rather than the other way around.

v25 'Strength and honor are her clothing; she shall rejoice in time to come.'

Weakness, irresponsibility, and indecency are her clothing. She churns with anxiety and fear about the future.

v26 'She opens her mouth with wisdom, and on her tongue is the law of kindness.'

Her words are foolish; people around her are negatively influenced by her cynicism and critical attitude. Bitterness and judgments about others regularly spew from her lips.

v27 'She watches over the ways of her household and does not eat the bread of idleness.'

She's stressed and concerned about all manner of things, but oblivious to the realities of what's happening inside her own heart and home. There, her exhaustion and stress boil over into laziness and inaction.

v28 'Her children rise up, and call her blessed; her husband also, and he *praises her.'*

Her children rise up and can't wait to get away from her. They curse her. Her husband also, and can't find anything good to say.

v29 *'Many daughters have done well, but you excel them all.'*

v30 *'Charm is deceitful, and beauty is passing, but a woman who fears the Lord, she shall be praised.'*

A woman who fears the Lord is to be praised. But this woman's charm is deceitful and her beauty is in vain.

v31 *'Give her of the fruit of her hands, and let her own works praise her in the gates.'*

Her hands are fruitless, and leave her nothing to enjoy or be praised for.

Are you prepared to live your lives according to these scriptures? If you are you will not only be in the will of God, but you will find the happiness and contentment that you desire.

Finally, I want to encourage you and your mate to seek the Lord together every day. Build such a strong bond together so Satan cannot come between you. **Isaiah 55:6; Jeremiah 29:11 – 13**

1 Peter 3:8-12
'Finally, all of you be like-minded, be sympathetic, love one another, be compassionate and humble.
Do not repay evil with evil or insult with insult. On the contrary, repay evil with blessing, because to this you were called so that you may inherit a blessing.
For, whoever would love life and see good days must keep their tongue from evil and their lips from deceitful speech.

They must turn from evil and do good; they must seek peace and pursue it.
For the eyes of the Lord are on the righteous and His ears are attentive to their prayer, but the face the Lord is against those who do evil.

My Journal

Ten Commandments For Those Who Have Been Previously Married

I will not live in the past

I will be responsible for my present and not blame my past

I will not feel sorry for myself indefinitely

I will assume my end of the blame for my marriage dissolvement

I will not try to reconcile my past and reconstruct my future with a quick new marriage

I will not spend all my time trying to convince my children how terrible and evil their departed parent is

I will learn all I can about being a one-parent family and get on with it

I will not make my children the victims of my past

I will ask others for help when I need it

I will ask God for the wisdom to bury yesterday, create today, and plan for tomorrow

Author Unknown

The Christian Marriage Review

1. What does **Galatians 3:28** say about the male and female?

2. According to **Genesis 2:18** (1st book in O.T) why did God create woman?

3. What are your feelings regarding submission to your husband?

4. Even though we read in the Bible that the husband is head of his wife, what must he do to show the Lord he is willing to guide his family toward God? **Colossians 3:19;** (12th book in N.T) **1 Peter 3:7** (21st book in N.T)

5. What does God say about the husband that does not provide for his family? **1 Timothy 5:8** (15th book in N.T)

6. What is **2 Corinthians 6:14 - 17** (8th book in N.T.) telling you?

7. From the list given in the text what areas do you need to improve to show your husband that you are worthy of his love?

8. Why is praying with your spouse important? **Matthew 18:20** (1st book in N.T)

9. What does God promise if we seek Him? **Jeremiah 29:11 - 13** (24th book in O.T)

Parenting God's Way

Raising children can be very challenging especially if you are a single parent. Just knowing the right way to discipline them, answering their questions, etc., can become frustrating especially when you see them trying to go in the wrong direction. I'm sure you have felt like pulling your hair out from time to time.

Single mothers not only have to be the sole provider, but they also have to be the disciplinarian, coach, caretaker, chef, cheerleader, counselor, protector, doctor, etc. If you have never had to face something like this alone it's hard to imagine how exhausting it can be.

Parenting is a great responsibility. Everyone has their own ideas of what will, and will not work. It's not always easy to find someone to go to for advice without feeling inadequate, that they are judging you and your way of parenting.

It should be every parent's commitment to teaching their children how to live a godly life and you do that by example. Let them know what you believe is right and wrong with the issues they will bring to you. If you do not want your children to smoke, drink alcohol, do drugs, etc., then you must not have them in your life.

If you have struggled with this in the past don't think you have failed but know you have done the best you could with the knowledge you had. It's never too late to change your parenting skills for both your and your child's benefit.

The Bible gives us some instructions on how to help our children grow into the adults that both you and God expect.

The first thing we should consider is dedicating our children to the Lord regardless of their age. **Psalms 127:3** *tells us that children are a heritage from the Lord.*

Mary and Joseph gave us an example when they dedicated Jesus. He was just a few weeks old when they presented Him to the Lord. When we dedicate our children to God we are giving our children back to our Heavenly Father. By doing this, you are showing God that you trust Him to fulfill whatever plan He has for your child.
Jeremiah 29:11 NIV
'For I know the plans I have for you,' declares the Lord, 'plans to prosper you and not to harm you, plans to give you hope and a future.'
Dedicating your child to God doesn't need to be done in a church setting, you can simply pray a sincere prayer to God, and He will hear you.

All children are precious in God's sight. Our children need to know that God loves them. **1 John 4:19; Luke 18:16**

He expects parents to raise their children according to His standards. Since most schools today show little or no acknowledgment or care for God or His commandments, it is our responsibility to begin our children's training while they are still in the crib.
You may think that it's too soon to start this, but we know how quickly they understand and mimic everything we do or say.

According to Paul's word in **Ephesians 6:4;** *as well as God's instructions in many Old Testament passages* **Genesis 18:19; Deuteronomy 6:6 - 7; Proverbs** *22:6, it is the responsibility of parents to give their children the upbringing that prepares them for lives pleasing to God. It is the family, not the church or church school that is primarily responsible for the Biblical and spiritual training of the children. Church and church schools only assist in parental training.*

Let your child see how important they are to you, that they are more important than your job, your friends, etc., Get involved in the things they do, at school, hobbies, and the like. They need to feel special and know you love them.

Help your children make wise choices and decisions especially when they are choosing their friends. These young people will have a certain amount of influence over your children.
Children must be made aware that living a moral life is of great importance not only to God but will greatly benefit them as they grow into adulthood. You do not want them to live with regrets, wishing that they had never done some of the things they did. **Galatians 5:19-21**

Some of their friends may not have been raised in a Christian home and they could encourage your child to experiment with drugs or alcohol. These are so prevalent in our society today.
When your child becomes old enough to spend the night at a friend's house do your homework and find out what their parents are like and if they have the same values you have. I don't want to instill fear in you, but you must be realistic. Not everyone you meet can be trusted with your child. They may look innocent enough on the outside but many

child predators are looking for their next victim. Don't let it be your child!!

It would be wonderful if we had a guarantee that all our hard work would pay off and our children would continually follow God throughout their lives. But we must realize that no matter how hard we try, there may be times we are influenced by the world and will give in to its temptations. **1 John** 2:15-17

If your child gets entangled in worldly things, don't allow Satan to temp you into thinking you did a poor job at raising them. We know that Satan shows up when we are in our weakest state and when we are too tired to fight.
So ignore his taunts, know you did the best job possible, and begin to pray for your child, believing that God will bring him back into the fold. Philippians 4:6

We should pray daily for our children, for protection from the evil one, for their health, that they excel at school, etc. Your prayers are very effective and can prevent bad things from happening to them.

Pray **Psalms** 121:3 - 8 over your children, making it personal by inserting their name where 'you' or 'your' is written. For example:

v.3 'He will not let <u>'child's name'</u> foot slip – He who watches over <u>'child's name</u> will not slumber nor sleep'.
And when you pray believe that God hears your prayers. **Matthew** 21:22

Now let's talk about discipline. This can be a touchy subject. Not everyone believes in spanking and would prefer to just talk to their children or use time-outs instead.
It is so important to teach your children to obey you. If they cannot learn this principle with their parents how will they learn to obey God and His Word? **Proverbs** 13:24

There is a fine line between discipline and abuse so we must be careful not to overstep the mark. There may be times when the things your children do or say make you so mad and frustrated that it would be so easy to lose your cool. This is the time we must be very careful not to cross that line and strike out at them.

Yelling and screaming at them won't help either. They will learn to turn a deaf ear to you and all you're doing is getting yourself worked up in a fit. Did you know that you can get into such a state that you lose all sense of reality? What are you accomplishing with this kind of attitude? It is better to walk away for a few minutes until you calm down before you deal with the situation.

Always try to talk to your child first before you set a punishment. They will probably have a reason why they did what they did. No matter how illogical it may sound to you, it may have seemed the right thing to them.

Always discipline with love, never out of anger. You must always be aware of your actions.

If the father is not living in the home but is still involved in their child's life they must not shirk their responsibilities of disciplining and teaching their children.

We must teach our children to love God and help them decide to accept Jesus as their personal Savior and to trust and follow Him.
Matthew 19:14
'Jesus said, 'let the little children come to Me. and so not hinder them, for the kingdom of Heaven belongs to such as these.'

Help them understand that God sees and hears everything they do and say, that He knows what is in their hearts. **Psalms 139:1-12**

We must teach our children the importance of prayer. Encourage them to pray every day for their family and friends, etc., as well as their own needs.

Make time every day to have family devotions with your children. This means praying with them and reading and studying the bible with them. If your child is too young to read by themselves then read those bible stories to them. Find bible storybooks with pictures, this will keep them interested. They even make washable books for babies. You will find many good resources online or at your local bible bookstore.

Praying and teaching them about Jesus will set an example to follow when they have a family of their own. **Deuteronomy 4:9**

Parents should not show favoritism to their children. You do not want them to grow up feeling unwanted, unloved, or not good enough. These negative feelings as well as jealousy can become deeply rooted inside all of us when we are made to feel inadequate. Instead, reach out to your child with love, compassion, kindness, humility, gentleness, and patience. **Colossians 3:12 – 14**

It is also important that we listen to our children, hug them often and even give them an understanding of their shortcomings.

There are a few rules that children should follow. The first is the hardest, that of obeying parents. We may want to have our way in matters but not everything is good for us. **Ephesians 6:1-3**
Parents put restrictions on their children when they are young for their benefit. They want to shield them from things that can be harmful to them.
From my own experience, as I grew into my teenage years I thought that my parents didn't understand what I was going through.
There truly is a generation gap between parents and their children but as the child matures into adulthood I hope they will understand where their parents were coming from.
Years later I wished I had listened to them about some of the things I did. I think most of us may have a little regret about those difficult years. Proverbs 1:8

Not only are children to obey their parents they must also respect them. **Ephesian 6:2**. The way they will learn respect is by watching you and see how you act toward others.

For example: If you are a single mother and you say hateful and disrespectful things against your ex in front of your children what do you think you are showing them? How do you think will they feel? He is their father. They may be scared to show much love for him, afraid you will get upset. Please don't do this to your children. Let them love you both without any repercussions. Don't make your child choose one parent over the other. That is not a healthy situation, and you may do more harm than good.

Arguing, talking back, or using bad language toward their parents is not showing respect. Colossians 3:20 'Children, obey your parents in all things, for this is pleasing to the Lord.'

Another area I feel very adamant about is the lack of manners seen in people today. It's not just young people who are guilty of this but also adults.
Many children today are not taught to say "please" and "thank you." They just do their own thing, grab what they want, and are never corrected for their behavior. It is the parent's responsibility to teach their children these principles. I understand that in most homes today both parents have to work, but that is no excuse. Don't leave it up to the babysitter to teach these things to your child, they may not have the same values you have.

Growing up in England, many years ago, manners were taught at a young age. Even as a small child, if you went to a shop to buy candy and you did not say please or thank you the shop assistant might refuse to serve you until you said those words.

It is also the parent's responsibility to teach their children how to act in public. If your child wants something and you say 'no,' and then your child throws a fit, don't give in. Take them to the bathroom and if talking to them doesn't work, give them a swat on their backside and continue shopping. If you give in, they will think that as soon as they cry or scream you will always give in. No matter how uncomfortable you may feel, stand your ground. Do not let your child dictate what you will or will not do. Remember, you are the parent. Act like it.

Lastly, I want to encourage you to have fun with your children. If you are raising them alone, you may be so absorbed with the difficulties of life that you forget to laugh and act silly around them. If money is an issue, find things in your location that you can take your children to that cost very little. Go to museums, the library, bowling, etc. even a walk in the park can be fun. Pack a picnic, ball, or frisbee and play with them.

Just doing little things like that means a great deal to children. Why? You are investing your time in your children, making memories, and showing them that they are important to you. So, lighten up parents! Go and have fun with your children, they will be grown before you know it.
Parenting Review/ Questions

Next to each statement place true or false

1. _____ Our children will never be influenced by the world.

2. _____ We can verbally attack our ex-husbands in front of our children anytime.

3. _____ We should pray for our children daily about their health, school, etc.

4. _____ Always discipline with love, never out of anger.

5. _____ Parents should not show favoritism to one child over another.

6. _____ It is important that parents listen to their children.

7. _____ Not only are children to obey their parents but they must also respect them. This is one of the ten commandments.

8. _____ It is never a problem to drink or do drugs with you children. God doesn't mind.

9. _____ Read **Proverbs 22:6,** Do you agree or disagree?

10. _____ Arguing, talking back, or using bad language towards their parents or others is showing respect.

11. _____ Do not let the child dictate what you will or will not do.

My Journal

Healing

There are a few areas I think I need to bring to your attention that are important to know, some of which I have already touched on. But I think it's worth writing these again.

We have all experienced hateful and hurtful things from others, and they can stay on our minds for a long time. It's hard to take control of our thoughts because our enemy Satan knows how to bring up our pasts and tries to manipulate us. He wants to immobilize us by keeping our focus only on the negative in our lives, instead of the positive. His goal is to get us into a state of depression and despair. There are times when we allow him to bind us up in chains through guilt, hopelessness, and anger.

Anger:

Anger at times is what flows from bitterness into an outburst of uncontrolled passion, frustration, and rage. Anger is an emotion that manifests [or shows] itself in shouting, abuse, and slander.

When things were going wrong in my life I would ask myself and God 'why is this happening to me'. Does that sound familiar?

Frustrated about your past, or angry about your present circumstances? Wanting to give up and throw in the towel? You may have battled with this for many years and at times it still creeps up on you now and again. When the ugliness of anger rear's up it can cause you to become judgmental and irritable towards your family, your friends, and yourself.

Uncontrollable anger can cause us to say and do things we would not normally do. But it just doesn't stop there. It continues to fester inside us until we are at the point of exploding, then every ugly thing comes flying out of our mouths. Many who have been victims of abuse become abusive to their families and themselves. The abused often become the abuser. We realize the hurtful things that were said or done, and now we wish that we have never said them.

Parents can sometimes scar their children with their words and actions. Satan continues to bring those memories into our minds to keep us bound and as a result, we cannot heal. So here is a tool to help you overcome your past. That tool is forgiveness.

Forgiveness:

Ephesians 4:31-5:2 NIV
'Get rid of all bitterness, rage, and anger, brawling and slander, along with every form of malice.
Be kind and compassionate to one another, forgiving each other, just as in Christ, God forgave you.
Follow God's example, therefore, as dearly loved children,
And walk in the way of love, just as Christ loved us and gave Himself up for us as a fragrant offering and sacrifice to God.'

You may say to yourself that it is impossible to forgive the one that hurt you the most. Since this type of pain goes in so deep, it is only natural that you feel forgiveness can never be achieved.

When a person has an unforgiving heart they put up a wall between them and God. The unforgiving person is like a person carrying heavy baggage. But that is where God comes in; He can help you overcome those feelings. Once you learn to forgive you can let go of that load you are carrying.

When we forgive, this stops Satan in his tracks. We are no longer a slave to feelings of anger, resentment, and brokenness. We have overcome the need to feel negative about the past and we have broken the hold that Satan has had on us for such a long time. Now, this doesn't mean you will forget everything that has happened to you but by forgiving, it will gradually help lessen the pain.

Jesus could have felt hatred towards those who nailed Him to the cross, but instead He asked His Father **'To forgive them, they know not what they do.' Luke 23:34'**

It is crucial that you learn to forgive yourselves for the things you did in your past. Are you still punishing yourselves because of your actions or the things that happened to you? If you continue to live in the past with feelings of shame, regret and even failure, your time of healing will be greatly increased. **Matthew 6:14 - 15**

Forgiveness is an easy word to say but not so easy to do. It doesn't just happen, it is something you may have to force yourself to do in the beginning. When you learn to forgive, a whole new set of emotions can rise to the surface. What has been brought into the light is no longer in the dark and Satan cannot use it against you anymore.

Only when you repent and ask the Lord Jesus into your life, will your healing begin. God may even draw you toward other hurting women who are also searching for the same healing power. Sharing your testimony, can not only help them overcome their pain but will also help them realize that they are not alone.

Confidence:

Many women have experienced abusive relationships and regardless of the type of abuse, lose all sense of confidence in themselves. We have been made to feel unworthy of any good thing that could come into our lives, that we are no better than the dirt under their shoes. But this is not true. We have value and are valuable to God.

We need to have confidence in God throughout our times of struggle. Do not look at the mountain of problems that stand before you but look at the magnitude of God and His ability to overcome those problems.

Matthew 6:26 NIV
'Look at the birds of the air; they do not sow or reap or store away in barns, and yet your Heavenly Father feeds them. Are you not much more valuable than they?'

Through the early stages of my relationship with Jesus Christ, He revealed things to me, protected me and guided me. In order to grow in my faith, God had to step back and give me the opportunity to learn how to walk on my own.

We do the same thing for our children as they are learning to walk. And just as we are there to catch them when they fall, I knew that my Lord was in the background ready to catch me if I would fall.

My Journal

Trust:

Have you ever been disappointed in people that you loved or still love, feeling rejected or betrayed? Or even felt like God let you down and wondered after a tragedy if you can still trust Him?

During the years that I was still a baby in Christ, I experienced those feelings toward God. I am not proud of the fact that I doubted Him, but we are all human and we all get scared from time to time. When I couldn't see God moving in my circumstances I became afraid and thought that He hadn't heard my prayers. I failed to put all my trust in Him.

God places us in situations to help us mature and grow in Him, to trust Him only, and to know that He is our source. He can do all things for all people if we would only trust and believe. So when your back is up against a wall, and you have nowhere to turn for help you must learn to trust God with all your circumstances.

I can look back on my life and see how He has protected me from people and situations that would have been painful had I gone ahead with my agenda.

Our faith becomes evident through our actions and words.
When people ask you how you are doing, do you say you are great even though your miracle has not yet happened, or do you moan and groan about how hard your life is? Which one of these scenarios shows your faith in God?
Do you strive to encourage others, helping them stay motivated in God? And in your prayer life, do you pray believing that God hears and will answer those prayers?

God has a plan for your life. You may not understand why you are suffering or struggling but one day you will look back and see how the Lord has worked things out and everything will make sense to you.

Jeremiah 29:11 - 14 NIV
'For I know the plans I have for you, declares the Lord, plans to prosper you and not to harm you, plans to give you hope and a future.
Then you call on Me and come and pray to Me, and I will listen to you. You will seek Me and find Me when you seek Me with all your heart. I will be found by you, declares the Lord, and will bring you back from captivity.'

I want to encourage you today to begin trusting in God, He is all you need to live a happy and victorious life.

Romans 15:13 NIV
'May the God of hope fill you with all joy and peace as you trust in Him, so that you may overflow with hope by the power of the Holy Spirit.'

Psalms 9:10 NIV
'Those who know Your name will trust in you, for You, Lord, have never forsaken those who seek you.'

My Journal

The Words We Speak

While flipping through the channels on the television, I came across a lady speaking about how the Lord can quickly give you a scripture when needed.

She was asked by her Pastor to speak for a few minutes to the children that gathered around the altar.

She sent up a quick prayer and the Lord gave her **Ephesians 4:29**.

She wasn't sure how she could apply this verse to the children but with God's help, she was able to minister to those children.

As she was speaking, the Holy Spirit prompted me to write some things down and for the next several days the Lord began to reveal other passages of scripture to me.

Ephesians 4:29 NIV
'Do not let any unwholesome talk come out of your mouths, but only what helps build others up according to their needs, that it may benefit those who listen.'

I want to write about the words we use.
Are the words we speak full of encouragement, or do they tear a person down?
Our lives are made up of blocks and these blocks are the words that have been spoken to us throughout our lifetimes.

It would be nice to say that we all had many blocks of fine words spoken to us throughout our years. But unfortunately, many of us since childhood have been told that we were no good, that we will never amount to anything, pointed out everything we have done wrong, or find fault in our every move.

You may have had people look down on you because you did not live in the right neighborhood, drive a new car, or wear the right clothes, These people make you feel like you do not measure up to their standards.

It's amazing how we can pour the bad into a person without realizing it by just being unaware or insensitive to their feelings.

We can also hurt someone unknowingly.

You may be speaking to a friend about another person. Even if it is a chance remark it could cause your friend to have a wrong opinion about that person. There is a fine line between innocent chatter and gossip.

The Bible tells us:

Leviticus 19:16 NIV
'Do not go about spreading slander among your people.'

Proverbs 11:13 NIV
'A gossip betrays a confidence, but a trustworthy person keeps a secret.'

Proverbs 16:28 NIV
'A perverse [or wicked] person stirs up conflict, and a gossip separates close friends.'

Proverbs 18:8 NIV
'The words of a gossip are like choice morsels; they go down to the in most parts.'

Proverbs 20:19 NIV
'A gossip betrays a confidence; so avoid anyone who talks too much.'

James 3:1 - 10 speaks about taming the tongue.

I don't think anyone wants to be labeled as a gossip. This is not a Godly attitude to have. Our words can influence people's attitudes towards others.
You have great power in your words so use them in the right way. There are times, as we go through trials that an encouraging word from someone is all we need to make it through the day.

1 Thessalonians 5:11 NIV
'Therefore encourage one another and build each other up.'

Hebrews 3:13 NIV
'But encourage one another daily, as long as it is called Today, so that none of you may be hardened by sin's deceitfulness.'

The writer of this verse tells us to 'encourage each other daily.' There is a reason for this. Our enemy attacks us every day!

Many times, with God's help, we can defeat the enemy.

But there are times when our situations look so bad that we feel like we cannot go on. We get to the point of giving up. We need help.

That's when friends and family can help. It costs us nothing to say a kind word to someone or offer to pray with them.

John 13:34 - 35 NIV
'A new command I give you: Love one another. As I have loved you, so you must love one another.
By this everyone will know that you are my disciples if you love one another.'

John 15:12 NIV
'My command is this: Love each other as I have loved you.'

As you can see by these two verses, Jesus Himself is commanding us to love each other.

Proverbs 17:17 NIV
'A friend loves at <u>all</u> times.'

Not just when it's convenient and things are going well but what comfort it gives to know that there is someone you can call in the middle of the night that will be with you and pray for you as long as you need them.

That's a true friend.

Romans 12:9 - 16 NIV
'Love must be sincere. Hate what is evil; cling to what is good.
Be devoted to one another in brotherly love. Honor one another above yourselves.
Never be lacking in zeal, but keep your spiritual fervor, serving the Lord.
Be joyful in hope, patient in affliction, faithful in prayer.
Share with the Lord's people who are in need. Practice hospitality.
Bless those who persecute you; bless and do not curse.
Rejoice with those who rejoice; mourn with those who mourn.
Live in harmony with one another. Do not be proud, but be willing to associate with people of low position. Do not be conceited.'

It's easy to say we will love each other at all times but it may not be the easiest thing to do. Especially to those who have intentionally hurt you.

As wives and mothers, we are constantly bombarded with everyone else's problems.
It's dad's job to fix things around the house but it's the mom who soothes the hurt feelings. We are expected to be the peacemakers of the family.

Sometimes we put so much pressure on ourselves to be the perfect wife, the perfect mother, and the perfect friend.

We do this by trying to stay in control of our feelings and never saying how we really feel.
Have you ever felt like crying out 'WHAT ABOUT ME AND MY NEEDS'?

These feelings get bottled up inside and if we are not careful they will begin to take root in our minds by way of anger, resentment, and sometimes feelings of inadequacy.

Our mind becomes Satan's playground. He will try to manipulate your every thought.

If this begins to happen your best defense is to take it to God.

It's OK to get upset occasionally but do not let these feelings control you.
Just know where they are coming from.

James 1:19 - 20 NIV
'My dear brothers and sisters, take note of this: Everyone should be quick to listen, slow to speak and slow to become angry,
Because human anger does not produce the righteousness that God desires.

Thank goodness our Father knows we are not perfect
and helps us overcome our weaknesses.

There may be times when you must rebuke someone, your children in particular, so be careful how you choose your words.
There are ways to get your point across without being brutal or crushing their spirit.

One young lady I heard had made scripture cards out of index cards and placed them in every room of her house to help her speak to her children in the right way.

We must be careful to keep the lines of communication open with the person we are upset with.
Many people haven't learned the principle of when to speak or when to be quiet.

It takes a special person to be the one to back away from a heated discussion.
But it's important to always ask yourself
'What Would Jesus Do' or 'How Would Jesus Handle This Situation?

Sometimes it takes a lot of self-discipline to keep quiet and not strike out at the other person.

When I get to a place where I could say hurtful things, I go into my study or whatever room that person is not in and talk to God and rebuke the enemy. I do not want to hurt them by blurting out all my negative feelings.

Walking away is not the easiest thing to do, as my flesh wants to stay and have the last word.

I'm sure you have ways of dealing with your frustrations.
Just be careful not to hurt anyone with your words.
Because once they are spoken you cannot retrieve them.

We should strive to have the following qualities in our life since we are Christian women:

Galatians 5:22 - 23 NIV
'But the fruit of the Spirit is love, joy, peace, forbearance (patience,) kindness, goodness, faithfulness,
gentleness, and self-control.

Colossians 3:12 - 14 NIV
Therefore, as God's chosen people, holy and dearly loved, clothe yourselves with compassion, kindness, humility, gentleness and patience.
Bear with each other and forgive one another if any has a grievance against someone. Forgive as the Lord forgave you.
And over these virtues put on love, which binds them all together in perfect unity.'

My question to you is this:
What are you pouring into others?

I want to challenge you to pour good words into those around you.
Become mentally aware of your words.
Stop before you speak.
Only speak words that will lift a person up and not tear them down.

I hope you will make some scripture cards and place them in your home or workplace and use it as a reminder to only speak good, kind, and encouraging words.

Luke 6:36 - 38 NIV
'Be merciful, just as your Father is merciful.
Do not judge, and you will not be judged. Do not condemn, and you will not be condemned. Forgive, and you will be forgiven.
Give, and it will be given to you. A good measure pressed down, shaken together, and running over will be poured into your lap. For the measure you use, it will be measured to you.'

Verse 36 says that we should be merciful, just as our Father is merciful.
So be merciful to everyone around you.
Judgment and condemnation are not what God expects from us.

We are to have the mind of Christ. And Christ is love.
Every morning we should dress with love, compassion, encouragement, and understanding, and then ask God who He wants us to speak to today.

When you sow these good seeds into others then God will reward you in like manner.
So be careful what and how you give.
'God, help us to always sow good seeds everywhere we go, and to everyone we meet.'

My Journal

THE JOURNEY

Matthew 28:19 - 20 NIV
'Therefore go and make disciples of all nations, baptizing them in the name of the Father and of the Son and of the Holy Spirit, And teaching them to obey everything I have commanded you. And surely I am with you always, to the very end of the age.'

God has commissioned all mature Christians to disciple and mentor young believers in Christ. Their goal is to help young Christians to daily grow closer to God through prayer and bible study and to help them weather the storms of life that they will encounter during their Christian walk.

To effectively disciple/mentor others there are standards that you must comply with.

- Living a holy and godly life is crucial for any Christian. You are the vessels that God wants to use to minister to others. He cannot use a dirty vessel. You should daily repent of any sin in your life and must make every effort to break the bondage that Satan has bound you in. Regardless of your sin whether drugs, alcohol, pornography, anger, bitterness, unforgiveness, etc., God wants to heal you and will help you overcome the enemy and his deceitful ways.

- Before you can begin the task of discipling/mentoring others, you must have an established firm spiritual foundation under you. This means you must have complete faith in the Lord Jesus Christ, that He will do what He has said He would do and will take care of your every need. We all go through trials at one time or another sometimes they can be devastating but since you know the Father and have learned to trust Him then you can be assured that He will lead you through the storm. Sometimes your trials may come about by your own making e.g. making bad decisions. Another reason you go through trials is brought about by our enemy Satan, he tries to get us to give up living for God because our situations look hopeless. And lastly, you may be going through a trial that the Lord has put on you. It is not to harm you but to help you grow in *faith, to reach out to Him in prayer and after you have gone through your testing time the Bible tells us in **Job 23:10** you will come forth as gold.*

- *God will use your talents and life experiences to minister to others. Sometimes as we go through different trials we wonder 'why me Lord?' Well, one reason could be that God will use your bad experiences to help others that will go through the same things. We tend to look at other people who are going through difficult times to see how they successfully get through them and this in turn encourages us. It can be hard to minister to someone going through a divorce, for example, if you have never gone through it yourself, you really cannot identify with their pain. But regardless of your own experiences, God will connect you with someone that you can minister to.*

- *There are no time limits when it comes to ministering to others. You may work with someone for just a short time and for one reason or another they will leave and go on their way. There may be others that you will minister to for a few years and still others will be with you for a lifetime.*
  Allow God to direct you concerning everyone that you minister to. Everything is in His timing. Do not try to outguess God or get in His way. To be successful in discipling/ mentoring you must stay closely connected to God and allow Him to direct you're every word and action.

- *Over the years I have found [through trial and error] not to become emotionally involved with those I was ministering to. It is like being on the outside looking in. You must stay objective in everything that is said. Before you meet with the person it is important to seek God in prayer and allow the Holy Spirit to speak through you because you do not always know the situation that person is in or even the questions they will ask.*

- Your committed prayer life is crucial for your success as well as the success of the person you are ministering to. You may need to teach them how to pray and praise God even in the midst of their storm. Allow them to see how important they are to you, how much you care. Have the same compassion for them as Jesus did.

    John 17:9 NIV
    'I pray for them. I am not praying for the world, but for those You have given me, for they are Yours.'

- Whenever we minister to people we must be prepared, gentle, and respectful.

I Peter 3:15 NIV
    'But in your hearts revere Christ as Lord. Always be prepared to give an answer to everyone who asks you to give the reason for the hope that you have. But do this with
gentleness and respect.'

- <u>**Prepared:**</u> As we have previously read we must be prepared to do the work of the Father. By seeking God in prayer and through His Word He makes us ready to minister. He will guide us to the right people and give us the words to say to help that person.

- <u>**Gentleness:**</u> Whatever else you have to do to minister to someone the most important is your love and compassion for them. As you read about Jesus in the New Testament you quickly see His love toward all people, especially those who are hurting. You are God's representative so you must take on the mind of Christ and present yourself as He would present Himself. Some things you must tell them may be hard for you to say and hard for them to receive, however, even in times like this, you can be assertive and present it in love where no offense is taken.

- <u>**Respectful:**</u> In everything you say and do always respect the person you are ministering to. In your eyes, they may have committed the worst sin imaginable but remember you are not there to judge that person but to help them. When ministering, remember, it's not about you. You are there to be the mouthpiece of God. Speak only the words He tells you to speak.

Philippians 2:3 - 5 NIV
'Do nothing out of selfish ambition or vain conceit, Rather, in humility value others above yourselves.
Not looking to your interests, but each of you to the interests of others.
In your relationships with one another, have the same mindset as Christ Jesus.'

- <u>**Encouragement:**</u> *Another thing we must do is to encourage those we minister to. We must always give them hope regardless of their circumstances. Sometimes you can use your own experiences and think back on the time when you were going through that exact thing. Do not be embarrassed to speak that out to them. Telling them how you overcame your particular problem, will in turn encourage them that they can also make it through.*

  It is important to memorize scripture or always keep your bible and your book of encouragement scriptures close at hand so you can show them through the Word what God says about that particular problem or to give them an encouraging Word from God.

Listed below are a few scriptures showing the different forms of encouragement.

<u>*God encourages us:*</u>

Isaiah 40:31 NIV
'But those who hope in the Lord will renew their strength. They will soar on wings like eagles; they will run and not grow weary, they will walk and not faint.'

The Bible encourages us:

Romans 15:4 NIV
'For everything that was written in the past was written to teach us, so that through the endurance taught in the Scriptures and the encouragement they provide we might have hope.'

We should encourage each other:

1 Thessalonians 4:18 NIV
'Therefore encourage one another with these words.'

<u>*Encourage those who are weak and afraid:*</u>

1 Thessalonians 5:14 NIV
'And we urge you, brothers, and sisters, warn those who are idle and disruptive, encourage the disheartened, help the weak, be patient with everyone.'

Encourage others not to sin:

Hebrews 3:13 NIV
'But encourage one another daily, as long as it is called 'Today,' so that none of you may be hardened by sin's deceitfulness.'

<u>*Encourage others to love:*</u>

Hebrews 10:24 NIV
'And let us consider how we may spur one another on toward love and good deeds.'

Proverbs 17:17 NIV
'A friend loves at all times.'

Philippians 2:1-2 NLT
'Is there any encouragement from belonging to Christ? Any comfort from His love? Any fellowship together in the Spirit? Are your hearts tender and compassionate?
Then make me truly happy by agreeing wholeheartedly with each other, loving one another, and working together with one mind and purpose.

God did not give us these gifts to keep to ourselves but to share with others. There is not one talent that is more important than another. It will require us to use all our talents together to get the job done. We do this with teamwork, meaning we do all things in unity. No gossiping, backbiting, etc.

I Corinthians 12:12 NIV
'Just as a body, though one, has many parts, but all its many parts form one body, so it is with Christ.'

1 Corinthians 12:27 NIV
'Now you are the body of Christ, and each one of you is a part of it.'

Since God gave us talents, we should use them for His glory.

And lastly, I want to add something I found many years ago. It spoke to my heart, and I hope it will touch you also. It's called

God's Love Letter To Me

My Child

You may not know Me, but I know everything about you: **Psalms** *139:1*

I know when you sit down and when you rise up: **Psalm** *139:2*

I am familiar with all your ways: **Psalms** *139:3*

Even the very hairs on your head are numbered: **Matthew** *10:29-31*

For you were made in My image: **Genesis** *1:27*

In Me you live and move and have your blessing: **Acts** *17:28*

For you are My offering: **Acts** *17:28*

I knew you even before you were conceived: **Jeremiah** *1:4-5*

I choose you when I planned creation: **Ephesians** *1:11-12*

You were not a mistake, for all your days are written in My book: *Psalms 139:15-16*

I determined the exact time of your birth and where you would live: **Acts** *17:26*

You are fearfully and wonderfully made: **Psalms** *139:14*

I knit you together in your mother's womb: **Psalms** *139:13*

And brought you forth on the day you were born: **Psalms** *71:6*

I have been misrepresented by those who don't know Me: **John** *8:41-44*

I am not distant and angry, I am the complete expression of love: **1 John** *4:16*

And it is My desire to lavish my love on you: **1 John** *3:1*

Simply because you are My child, and I am your Father: **1 John** *3:1*

I offer you more than your earthly father ever could: **Matt** *7:11f*

For I am the perfect Father: **Matthew** *5:48*

Every good gift that you receive comes from My hand: **James** *1:17*

For I am your provider and I meet all your needs: **Matthew** 6:31-33

My plan for your future has always been filled with hope: **Jeremiah** 29:11

Because I love you with an everlasting love: **Jeremiah** 31:3

My thoughts toward you are countless as the sand on the seashore: **Psalms** 139:17-18

And I rejoice over you with singing: **Zephaniah** 3:17

I will never stop doing good to you: **Jeremiah** 32:40

For you are My treasured possession: **Exodus** 19:5

I desire to establish you with all My heart and all My soul: **Jeremiah** 32:41

And I want to show you great and marvelous things: **Jeremiah** 33:3

If you seek Me with all your heart, you will find Me: **Deuteronomy** 4:29

Delight in Me and I will give you the desires of your heart: **Psalms** 37:4

For it is I that gave you those desires: **Philippians** 2:13

I can do more for you than you could possibly imagine: **Ephesians** 3:20

For I am your greatest encourager: **2 Thessalonians** 2:16-17

I am also the Father who comforts you in all your troubles: **2 Corinthians** 1:3-4

When you are broken-hearted, I am close to you: **Psalms** 34:18

As a shepherd carries a lamb, I have carried you close to My heart: **Isaiah** 40:11

One day I will wipe away every tear from your eyes: **Revelation** 21:3-4

And I will take away all the pain you have suffered on this earth: **Revelation** 21:3-4

I am your Father, and I love you even as I love My son Jesus: **John** 17:23

For in Jesus, My love for you is revealed: **John** 17:26

He is the exact representation of My being: **Hebrews** 1:3

He came to demonstrate that I am for you, not against you: **Romans** 8:31

And I tell you that I am not counting your sins: **2 Corinthians** 5:18-19

Jesus died so that you and I could be reconciled: **2 Corinthians** 5:18-19

His death was the ultimate expression of My love for you: **I John** *4:10*

I gave up everything I loved that I might gain your love: **Romans** *8:31-32*

If you receive the gift of My son Jesus, you receive Me: **1 John** *2:23*

And nothing will ever separate you from My love again: **Romans** *8:38-39*

Come home and I will throw the biggest party Heaven has ever seen: **Luke** *15:7*

I have always been your Father and will always be your Father: Ephesians 3:14-15

My question is **"Will you be My child":** *John 1:12-13*

I am waiting for you: **Luke** *15:11-32*

Love,

Your Father, Almighty God

Author Unknown

My Journal

Bio

I was born in Ipswich, England to wonderful parents and I am the oldest of five children. I moved to Texas USA in 1972. December of that year while watching an Oral Roberts Crusade on the TV, the Lord began to stir my spirit. Not understanding what was happening to me, I was told I need to find a church to attend, which I did in Lubbock Texas. In school, I had learned the stories about Jesus but never knew I needed a personal relationship with Him. That was the beginning of my walk with the Lord.

I knew absolutely nothing about being a Christian, so it was trial and error most of the time. I believe that is the reason God gave me the desire to minister to new Christians. I didn't want to see others go through as many pitfalls as I had.

I live in Arkansas with my wonderful husband Tim. I have 2 children, 4 grandchildren, and 7 great-grandchildren. I love to write, read, and enjoy working in my garden.

God has been so gracious to me and has walked with me through the years. I aspire to live Proverbs 3:5-6

'Trust in the Lord with all your heart and lean not on your understanding; in all your ways acknowledge Him and He shall direct your path'.

Made in the USA
Columbia, SC
24 January 2023